Living in Sodom Today

LIVING IN SODOM TODAY

© 2003 by Dr. Larry Spargimino

Unless otherwise indicated, Bible quotations are taken from the King James Version.

Printed in the United States of America

Published by
Bible Belt Publishing
P.O. Box 100 ▪ Bethany, OK 73008
(405) 789-1222 ▪ (800) 652-1144

ISBN 0-9744764-2-0

Living in Sodom Today

The Reality and the Rage

by

Dr. Larry Spargimino

Contents

Introduction

This is a difficult topic. Writing a book on homosexuality may be likened to swimming against the current. What current? The current of confusion created by the liberal media and the politically-correct crowd.

It is also a difficult topic because some of the material may be considered offensive by some. I make no apology for what the Bible says about homosexuality. But the offense may be occasioned not just by the Bible, but by some of the more repugnant aspects of the gay lifestyle and the diseases that are associated with it.

I have deliberately tried to not be overly graphic. Yet gay sex is more than two people of the same gender holding hands. Many people are naively unaware of this, nor are they aware of the intense push by those supportive of the homosexual agenda to gain acceptance for these hurtful practices.

In an attempt to see the whole picture I have read the fruits of Christian commentary and study on this topic, but I have also felt obliged to consult sources written by homosexuals. Much of the material cannot be quoted in a volume such as this. My desire is to inform without corrupting. Hopefully, I have included enough descriptive material to alert the reader of the dangers associated with the homosexual lifestyle without describing those practices in detail. No doubt, some readers will think that I have gone too far, others that I have not gone far enough. I have sought the Lord's guidance in this and have peace that I have walked what is a fine line.

Why write a book on homosexuality? Because this is a topic concerning which we dare not be in ignorance. On every front homosexuals are gaining victories. They are spending millions and have infiltrated the media and high places of government. We cannot be in ignorance of an issue that could change the very fabric of society as we know it.

Homosexuals are deliberately seeking to increase the acceptance of the homosexual lifestyle on practically every front: in the courts, in the classrooms, and in the entertainment industry. They have persuaded many politicians that they need special laws and legislation to guarantee their civil liberties. But they want more. They realize that the homosexual lifestyle will never be fully accepted by a large segment of society unless they can exert a considerable amount of influence in the heterosexual community and show that there is really nothing wrong with their lifestyle.

Being fully cognizant of the opposition to homosexuality in Christian circles, activists are actively seeking to neutralize this opposition. One of their strategies is to use all of the legal tools available. On August 13, 1993, homosexual activist Mel White appeared on "Larry King Live" and sounded a note that has been ignored, but one that should resound loud and clear:

> We [homosexual activists] have gone underground and we have people in every one of the Religious Right's organizations. We're on their mailing lists. We're reading everything they're putting out. We think the words from their mouths trickle down into violence. And when our evidence reaches a critical mass, we're going to use the best attorneys in this country to bring a class action suit in 50 states to have it stopped.[1]

In addition to the legal and political arenas, homosexuals are working in the religious arena as well. They are trying to show that the homosexual lifestyle is perfectly consistent with the Christian life and that Scripture does not give a blanket condemnation of homosexual relations, only certain kinds of homosexual relations. I was amazed at what they have done to the Scriptures! Gay Bible exposition has twisted Scripture, but it has done so in a careful and clever way that often makes their interpretations plausible.

They are also trying to rewrite history. To this end, activists seek to show that Christian tradition has been decidedly homophobic, but that when the original documents of the Christian faith are carefully examined, the objections quickly disappear. Those who are pushing hard in this area are called revisionists. "Their goal is to revise—or redefine—the historic teaching of the Christian church regarding sexual behavior."[2]

Though all of this may be troubling to some, I believe that God is doing a great work of separation in these last days. Controversy has a way of dividing and making manifest truth from error, light from darkness. We mustn't think that the overwhelming victories that gay activists seem to be winning in the legal and political arenas are omens of evil. "For there must be also heresies among you," we read in 1 Corinthians 11:19, "that they which are approved may be made manifest among you." The apostle was convinced that some division in the assembly would occur no matter what, if only to bring to light those who are defenders of the truth. Though the apostasy be ever so great, God will always have His faithful remnant.

I have sought to avoid overstating what homosexual activists are hoping to achieve and, in order to avoid the charge "we really don't believe that," I have sought to quote them extensively. I have also sought to avoid the trite clichés and stereotypes that are often flung about to no avail. The use of such cliches discredits those who use them and conveys the message that the writer does not really have anything of substance to say.

I submit this volume in the hope that Christian people might know how to deal with the challenges and claims of homosexual activism. It would be wonderful, too, if some who are entrapped in this destructive lifestyle came to know the freedom and liberty that is in Christ Jesus.

PART I

The Reality

CHAPTER 1

"I didn't realize we've come so far."

This know also, that in the last days perilous times shall come. For men shall be lovers of their own selves . . . Without natural affection."

—2 Timothy 3:1–3

In Matthew 13 Jesus Christ tells a series of parables dealing with the advance of the Kingdom of Heaven, as well as the advance of the kingdom of darkness. He tells a story about a man who went out and sowed good seed. In verse 25 Jesus says: "But while men slept, his enemy came and sowed tares among the wheat."

While most Christians have been soundly asleep, the homosexual agenda has been advanced by committed gays who have shown a remarkable determination for "winning" this aspect of the culture war. How ever you feel about this issue you must admit that homosexuals deserve an "A" for effort and for persistence. The following is a summary of what has been happening in the gay rights movement in a little more than a century.

1895—Famous writer, Oscar Wilde, is convicted for "gross indecency between males." Some in the community of artists and writers complain of such harsh treatment.

1924—The first formal U.S. gay-activist group is founded in Chicago.

1969—Patrons of Stonewall Inn resist a police raid in what's considered the birth of the gay-rights movement.

1975—Former NFL player Dave Kopay announces he's gay and becomes the first professional athlete to do so.

1977—Anita Bryant mounts a national crusade to block so-called gay rights.

1986—The Supreme Court rules in the *Bowers* case that sodomy is a crime.

1987—ACT UP is born, taking up the fight against AIDS.

1993—The military adopts the "don't ask, don't tell" guideline, though this is never made official policy for the armed forces; thousands of gay rights activists march on Washington.

1996—The U.S. Supreme Court rules that gays enjoy equal rights under the Constitution.

1997—Ellen DeGeneres' TV character has a "coming out."

2000—Vermont allows gay couples to form civil unions.

2001—Federal judge upholds law banning gay adoption.

2003—An openly gay Episcopal bishop is elected in New Hampshire.[1]

How Society Has Come to Change Its View of Homosexuality

While there are still large numbers of Christians, and others, who do not see anything positive about the homosexual lifestyle nor do they have any desire to ever accept it as normative, many people have become more open to it and less willing to see it as abnormal.

Much of this shift in the general perception of homosexuality has been done under the influence of medical and psychiatric "experts." In a society that gives great credence to the conclusions of the "experts" this was a prudent strategy that has shown itself to be highly effective. After all, isn't it better to let the "experts" guide our views rather than religion and prejudice?

In his book *Homosexuality and the Politics of Truth*, Jeffrey Satinover, M.D., traces some significant developments to the early 1970s when "gay liberators" were seeking to push for new legislation and greater tolerance. Part of their strategy was to influence the American Psychiatric Association (APA) to redefine and destigmatize homosexuality. A brief history of the rapidity of the changes that were brought about, and how these changes came to take place, will show the effectiveness of the plan.

In 1963 the New York Academy of Medicine, concerned that there seemed to be an increasing acceptance of homosexuality, charged its Committee on Public Health to investigate the issue. The committee researched the subject, consulted among themselves, and reported that "homosexuality is indeed an illness. The homosexual is an emotionally disturbed individual who has not acquired the normal capacity to develop satisfying heterosexual relations." The committee also noted that "some homosexuals have gone beyond the plane of defensiveness and now argue that deviancy is a 'desirable, noble, preferable way of life.'"[2]

This was a significant conclusion in that it affirmed and reaffirmed the committee's views on homosexuality. Consequently, the committee saw no reason to change its original conclusions regarding homosexuality. However, just ten years later, in 1973, the APA voted to remove homosexuality from its official list of psychiatric illnesses. How did this amazing turnaround occur?

Satinover, who is a former Fellow in Psychiatry and Child Psychiatry at Yale University and past William James Lecturer in Psychology and Religion at Harvard, comments: "Normally a scientific consensus is reached over the course of many years, resulting from the accumulated weight of many properly designed studies. But in the case of homosexuality, scientific research has only now just begun, years *after* the question was decided. . . . The APA vote to normalize homosexuality was driven by politics, not science."[3]

In the ten year period between 1963 and 1973 homosexual activists were hard at work seeking to get a change in status for their chosen lifestyle. At one meeting held in 1970 an eminent psychiatrist was presenting a paper on homosexuality. He was abruptly challenged by someone who stated: "I've read your book, Dr. Bieber, and if that book talked about black people the way it talks about homosexuals, you'd be drawn and quartered and you'd deserve it."[4]

This single statement is highly revealing. It demonstrates that the playing field had now changed. The opposition to the acceptance of the homosexual lifestyle was now being muzzled on the basis of it being mean-spirited. "Talking about homosexuals" had now been made equivalent to "talking about black people."

When the APA voted on changing its classification of homosexuality in 1973 a majority of its members who responded voted to change the classification of homosexuality. This, however, is only part of the story. Only one-third of the membership responded and had their views counted. The vote was not representative of the will of the body. Four years after the change in classification the journal *Medical Aspects of Human Sexuality* reported the results of a survey it had conducted. The survey demonstrated that 69 percent of the psychiatrists disagreed with the decision and still considered homosexuality a disorder. One researcher concluded that "the result was not a conclusion based upon an approximation of scientific truth as dictated by reason, but was instead an action demanded by the ideological temper of the times."[5]

This conspiracy of evil has brought conflict to the home and classroom. Activists are seeking to get their views into the classroom under the descriptive titles of "Health Education" or "Sex Education." Explicit, "non-judgmental" teaching on sexuality is used to expose children to homosexuality in all of its forms. Students are repeatedly warned to avoid bigotry and to not let their family's religious values color their thinking. Hate crimes and homophobia, they are told, are the fruits of outmoded sexual values that are built on a Sunday school mentality.

Fads and fashions are promoted through clothing and hairstyles associated with the gay culture. TV programs, interviews, and books showing how nice homosexuals are have part and parcel in this new psychosexual curriculum.

All of this helps the advancing homosexual agenda by desensitizing children to the evils of homosexual promiscuity. Parents who would even try to voice disapproval are treated like right-wing weirdos. Unbelievable conflict is introduced into the home when teenage boys and girls are correctly prohibited by their parents from "dressing like that." Teenagers, and even young children, retaliate by sulking and retreating to their rooms. "I don't like you!" the teenager shouts as he or she slams the door and leaves the room. "I want to leave and never come back!" Billy shouts at his father. Mom who is distressed with the continual haggling over fads and fashions, friends and curfews, thinks that maybe she and her husband have been too hard on Billy. After all, almost all of Billy's friends are dressing like that and even Billy's father wears some of the clothing that has been seen on pro-gay programs.

The homosexual cause is given further assistance in the public schools by radical groups such as Planned Parenthood and others that lobby for abortion services, condom distribution, and AIDS education. Parents who object to these alleged public health initiatives are depicted as lovers of ignorance who are in denial of the fact that "all teenagers do it." None of this, however, should surprise anyone. It is just symptomatic of the fact that American public education is driven by moral values.

Homosexual activists are continuing their work. They are not satisfied with "mere" tolerance; they want mass acceptance. At a gay rights march on Washington in 1987, Jeff Levi stated:

> We are no longer seeking just a right to privacy and a protection from wrong. We also have a right—as heterosexual Americans already have—to see government and society affirm our lives. Until our relationships are recognized in the law—in tax laws and government programs to affirm our relationships, then we will not have achieved equality in American society.[6]

Activists will stop at nothing, including litigation. Your free speech and my free speech are in great jeopardy. When legal developments provide new and more comprehensive avenues for litigation, there will always be lawyers and litigants who will take advantage of these new possibilities. Christians can expect more litigation. "There is no shortage of potential plaintiffs—individuals offended by Christians or Christianity—and there will be no shortage of lawyers to take their cases."[7]

The recent Supreme Court *Lawrence v. Texas* decision, which struck down the Texas anti-sodomy law, will undoubtedly embolden homosexuals to go to court. They now have good reason for believing that the judicial tyranny that is twisting the Constitution will also guarantee their success. As one observer put it, the *Lawrence* decision "actually expands the homosexual lobby's ability to use federal power to reconfigure private institutions."[8]

Convincing People That Homosexuality Is "the Gift of God"

The homosexual agenda has education—or I should say "re-education"—high on its list of priorities. People need to change their thinking about homosexuality, especially Christian people. This intended shift in values is to be accomplished in a threefold manner.

1. Attack the scriptural objections to homosexuality.

Conservative Christians appeal to certain key scriptures in both the Old and New Testaments. We are all familiar with the account of Sodom and Gomorrah, Paul's indictment of homosexuality in Romans 1, and his promise that the grace of God has and can change gays as found in 1 Corinthians 6:9–11. Homosexual revisionists attack traditional interpretations of these and other Scriptures and seek to show the alleged fallacy of such interpretations. Rather than attacking Scripture they make it seem that they are upholding Scripture, but attacking biased and erroneous interpretations of Scripture.

If any of my readers have ever witnessed to a Jehovah's Witness, Mormon, or other cultist who claims biblical authority for their views, you will be familiar with this approach. Evangelicals who correctly hold to the doctrine of the Trinity will be told by cultists that such a doctrine is really a holdover from the Roman Catholic Church, and that when Scripture is properly understood you will see that Jesus is only godlike, but certainly not God.

Homosexual revisionists do the same thing with those texts that are used to show that homosexuality is sin. They will seek to point out that traditional understandings of the biblical text are really marred by personal prejudice or by a misunderstanding of what the text *really* says. They will argue, for example, that when a biblical text is properly understood it is only condemning *abusive* homosexual relationships or *uncommitted* homosexual relationships, but not all such relationships.

To make their point revisionists will argue that some of the well-known people of the Bible—David and Jonathan, Ruth and Naomi, Paul and Timothy—probably engaged in committed homosexual acts.

In attacking the scriptural objections to homosexuality revisionists will claim that the account of the doom of Sodom and Gomorrah has been manipulated and wrested by heterosexuals. In 1955 Anglican priest Derrick Sherwin Bailey advanced the novel idea that the verb "to know" in Genesis 19:5 has been traditionally misunderstood. When the crowd demanded that Lot bring his two visitors out "that we may know them," this does not mean that the men wanted to have sexual relations with Lot's guests but that the men of Sodom merely wanted to "get acquainted with" these men as a token of hospitality, and also to examine their "passports" to ascertain whether or not they were enemies and posed a threat to the community.

Bailey pointed out that the verb "to know" (*yada*) appears 943 times in the Old Testament Scriptures and that in only about ten of the occurrences of the word does it mean "to know someone intimately." Sodom's sin, according to this view, was that the men of the city were violent in their efforts to get acquainted with the visitors and that their real sin was inhospitality.

Still other revisionists have argued that the men of Sodom were guilty of homosexual rape which even homosexual revisionists will admit is wrong. God's judgment, however, was for homosexual rape but not for homosexuality is the claim. However, as De Young observes, "Inhospitality did characterize the Sodomites because they pursued homosexual attack. There is a false dichotomy being made by the revisionists between inhospitality and sexual sin. The Sodomites were violent *because of* their homosexual lusts."[9]

But what about the argument that in most cases "to know" does not mean sexual intimacy? No doubt, the word is frequently used for mere cognizance and can mean "to be acquainted with." However, in the context of the early chapters of Genesis it does have sexual connotations:

> "And Adam *knew* Eve his wife; and she conceived, and bare Cain" (Gen. 4:1).
> "And Cain *knew* his wife; and she conceived, and bare Enoch" (Gen. 4:17).
> "And Adam *knew* his wife again; and she bare a son" (Gen. 4:25).

The repeated use of "to know" for the purpose of indicating physical relations in the early chapters of Genesis establishes a meaning and precedent in the book and argues for the legitimacy of this understanding of the term in Genesis 19:5. Reinforcing this interpretation is Lot's response to the request of the crowd, as found in verses 6 and 7: "And Lot went out at the door unto them, and shut the door after him, And said, I pray you, brethren, do not so *wickedly*." The kind of "knowing" these men were anticipating was viewed by Lot as being "wicked," hardly a descriptive word for inhospitality. Moreover, Lot's solution to the need of these men was to offer his virgin daughters "which have not known man" (vs. 8). Is there any reasonable doubt that more than "checking out their passports" is intended here?

The twisting of Scriptures is a very common strategy. The reader will find a whole chapter, chapter seven, devoted to this.

2. Attack the historical and societal objections to homosexuality.
Revisionists first try to discredit the traditional biblical objections to homosexuality, and after doing that they move on to seek to demolish the historical and societal objections.

Many of the church fathers and later Christian thinkers were opposed to homosexuality. This is admitted by revisionists, but they try to show that the fathers did so out of their own personal bias, not because of any mandate in the Word of God.

Some revisionists point out that the Greeks had a very open-minded attitude toward homosexuality, and that Greek society was one of the most open to same-sex relationships. The Greeks even told stories of homosexual activities among their gods.

Yet while this is all true, it is not the whole story. Certain Greek thinkers, such as Plato and Aeschines, "called for restraining same-gender sexual behavior."[10] It is not true that there was universal approval for homosexual practices in the ancient world. While revisionists would seek to make homosexual activities normal and acceptable, "no known society has endorsed or given unrestricted freedom to partake of all forms of homosexual behavior. In addition, no society in all of recorded history has given protected minority status to homosexuals."[11]

In 1986 the United States Supreme Court, in *Bowers v. Hardwick*, upheld the anti-sodomy law in the state of Georgia. The Georgia law allows the state to prohibit sodomy even when it occurs in private between consenting adults. Moreover, "the court declared that there is no right to homosexual activity in the Constitution of the United States."[12] While there is plenty of documentation to show that many generations of thinkers have seen homosexuality as being undesirable, such cannot be said about the new openness and acceptance. It is totally novel and without general historical precedent. The Supreme Court justices who voted to strike down the Texas anti-sodomy law were clearly sticking their necks out and moving in a new direction, supported neither by Scripture, history, nor tradition.

But what about the societal objection that homosexuals have a high suicide rate and are often guilty of abusing their same-sex partner? Is that a valid argument against society's endorsement of homosexuality?

Revisionists have a ready-made response: Homosexuals are despised and hated by a homophobic society. The high incidence of suicide and abuse is due not to the homosexual lifestyle, but to the stress of living in a narrow-minded anti-gay world. Revisionists claim that stress caused by a homophobic world is to blame.

This argument, however, won't "hold water." Society is becoming increasingly more tolerant of gays. They are advancing into every career and field of endeavor including industry, commerce, politics, law, and public education. Rather than being uniformly persecuted they are gaining the public acceptance that they so desperately crave. Contrary to what is claimed by the revisionists the physical and mental health problems stem from the lifestyle, not from those who oppose the lifestyle.

The "patron saint" of the revisionists was the late Yale professor John Boswell who wrote *Christianity, Social Tolerance, and Homosexuality.* Revisionists often preface a statement by saying, "Boswell says. . . ." This is supposed to have the force of an irrefutable statement.

Boswell's basic idea is that following the dissolution of the Roman Empire there was a generally tolerant attitude toward homosexuality in Europe in the Middle Ages. He argues that the civil and ecclesiastical pronouncements against homosexuality did not reflect the views of the majority of Christians. Boswell, who was openly gay, died of AIDS in 1994.[13]

While revisionists like Boswell have marshaled lots of historical and ecclesiastical information to make their point, they fail to do so. I believe that while they are good at giving history its proper "spin," objective historical reporting is of no interest to "spin doctors."

3. Attack the theological objections to homosexuality.
Revisionists stress that God is love. They believe that love is a "liberating ethic" demanding that the local church accept gays and allow them to participate fully in membership and leadership.

Yet, this is not without problems, because it creates a false dichotomy between love and law, as if love and law have nothing to do with each other. Such is not true. Biblical love is responsible love guided by the dictates of Scripture. In fact the Bible says, "For this, Thou shalt not commit adultery, Thou shalt not kill, Thou shalt not steal, Thou shalt not bear false witness, Thou shalt not covet; and if there be any other commandment, it is briefly comprehended in this saying, namely, Thou shalt love thy neighbor as thyself. Love worketh no ill to his neighbor: therefore love is the fulfilling of the law" (Rom. 13:9–10). Notice it says that love fulfills the law. The text does not say that love abolishes the law. The only way that homosexuality could ever hope to be considered acceptable in God's sight would be if Scripture said "love abolishes the law."

Scriptural love is a wonderful ethic. "Love worketh no ill to his neighbor." Homosexuality cannot be a loving act because homosexual relations brings much ill to one's neighbor.

Revisionists make a subtle shift in the language of the Bible. First John 4:8 says: "God is love." For them it reads: "Love is God." This is idolatry and has no sanction from Scripture. God never says this in Scripture. Because we are all fallen sinners if "love is God" we could easily justify our sinful proclivities and claim that we are walking in the path of love. If "Love is God" then I could easily justify murder, adultery, robbery, lying, and a whole host of evils. The Bible never says "Love is God" because it would ruin character and conduct.

Revisionists argue that there are no theological objections to a *committed* homosexual relationship. Just as God only condemns irresponsible heterosexual relations outside of the marriage covenant, so God only condemns irresponsible homosexual relations outside of a "gay marriage covenant." If two men, or two women, live together and are faithful to the relationship and find sexual satisfaction only within that relationship, that is fine with God, so they say.

However, there simply is no parallel. There are many duties that husbands and wives have to each other, but we NEVER read of parallel duties between partners in a same-sex relationship. While God enjoins husbands and wives to not deny each other and to render "due benevolence" (1 Cor. 7:1–5), the Bible NEVER makes the same comment regarding homosexual couples. In whatever form it appears, homosexuality is uniformly and consistently condemned by Scripture.

Homosexuals speak about committed homosexual "marriages" and about how same sex parents can raise children. But are there committed homosexual "marriages"? Dailey writes:

Studies indicate that the average male homosexual has hundreds of sex partners in his lifetime. It is difficult for even "committed" homosexual partners to part with this pattern of promiscuous behavior, which many homosexuals consider to be an integral part of the "gay lifestyle." A. P. Bell and M. S. Weinberg, in their classic study of male and female homosexuality, found that 43 percent of white male homosexuals had sex with five hundred or more partners, with 28 percent having 1,000 or more sex partners.[14]

These are shocking statistics. They challenge the contention that there is such a thing as a committed homosexual marriage or that same-sex partners remain monogamous. These statistics also show that there is sound reason for denying adoption privileges to same-sex couples. Based on the above statistics it is possible that two male homosexuals who are trying to raise children could have sexual relations with hundreds of partners. Is this the kind of situation that is conducive to raising healthy, emotionally-stable children?

I am certainly not trying to be mean-spirited in this book, but such questions cannot be avoided. Society has a vested interest in legislating against certain kinds of behavior. Homosexual "marriages" in which the partners have adoption rights bring children into unbelievably trying circumstances.

The Strategy Unfolds

Most of my readers have seen gay pride marches on the television. Many of the participants seem quite undisciplined. This may be true, but the organizers are following a carefully-constructed plan.

In their excellent book *The Homosexual Agenda: Exposing the Principal Threat to Religious Freedom Today*, authors Alan Sears and Craig Osten describe how homosexual activists are taking us to their goal of unbridled sexual behavior.

Stage One: Establish—
In this stage several homosexuals with a bent toward activism, establish a gay community so that they can have a larger role in society and bring about a policy change.

Stage Two: Organize—
Once a community is established the members seek closer, formal ties with each other for the sake of making their ideas heard. At this point they develop a "game plan" for the implementation their strategy.

Stage Three: Mobilize—
The group pools their resources and actually puts their strategy into action. Meetings are held, officers are chosen, and responsibilities are delegated to worthy and capable individuals within the group.

An important part of the mobilizing stage is to malign those who oppose their agenda and philosophy. They do this by labeling them as "intolerant" and "hateful." At this stage Scripture is reinterpreted to show that the Bible does not condemn "loving homosexual relationships."

Stage Four: Legitimize—
Once homosexuality is destigmatized, it is now possible to view homosexual activity as a personal choice, not a fixed moral issue. Society can now be reprogrammed so that society is now willing to give special privileges and rights to make up for the so-called injustices of the past.[15]

All around America, in Europe, Asia, and even the Middle East, this strategy is unfolding with telling effect. Homosexuals are growing in number, finances, and political clout. No stone is left unturned, no group is left untouched. Perhaps the most important group from the standpoint of winning the culture war, and most vulnerable, are the children. It is to this group that we now turn.

CHAPTER 2

Children Under Attack

. . . but bring them up in the nurture and admonition of the Lord

—Ephesians 6:4

Parents, Do You Know What They Are Teaching Your Children?

Marin County, California, is located just north of the Golden Gate Bridge. It's a lovely area of friendly people, rolling hills, and a drenching Pacific fog that blankets everything at certain times of the year. But more than fog is creeping into the community.

When one mom and dad sat down at the dinner table with their fourth-grade son, they weren't ready for what they heard. The little boy told his parents that he and his classmates had been learning slogans like, "I'm gay and it's okay." He said: "We learned that there are all kinds of families, including two mommies and two daddies." The boy also shared some of the words he had learned for the first time that day at school: "homosexual," "lesbian," and "faggot."

Just down the street a third-grade girl asked, "Daddy, am I a lesbian? I like girls better than boys."[1] There is a steady bombardment of young people with ideas and concepts that throw their sexuality and gender into question.

In his book *A Season For Justice,* Christian attorney David French tells how American public schools are now in a mad rush to indoctrinate students into the gay lifestyle. In one case, involving a public school in the suburbs of Boston, Massachusetts, a mother joined with concerned parents to make an urgent appeal to the governor's office. The scenario described below is becoming all too common.

Her son had started to attend meetings of the local high school's Gay/Straight Alliance club. When the mother discovered that the club watched at least one R-rated video of two boys "having a love affair," she was alarmed. The mother had also discovered upsetting handouts in her son's room. The boy's personality was beginning to change. With alarm, she came to the conclusion that he was becoming involved in a homosexual affair.

The mother complained to the principal, but he would not investigate the club. Though she tried to get other officials to investigate, none would. Instead, it was suggested that maybe she was "homophobic." The mother finally went to the governor of Massachusetts, Paul Celucci, but he refused to speak with her, nor would anyone from his office. The mother finally gained the ear of a public health official, but later the official would not return the calls he received. No wonder. Local and state governments are using tax dollars to fund explicit advocacy of the homosexual lifestyle and using graphic materials to get their work done. French asks:

> Why would the mother of a possibly gay student appeal to the governor of a state for help with a problem club at a local school? The answer is simple. Each year, the governor budgeted $1.5 million for the "Governor's Commission for Gay and Lesbian Youths." This commission is comprised primarily of gay activists and has used state money to lobby successfully over 180 Massachusetts schools to accept Gay/ Straight Alliance clubs.[2]

Parents who are trying to deal with this flood of gay-laced material are being stopped at every point. When parents complain, principals simply sigh. When confronted with charges that there is a GSA club in their school holding meetings they say something like, "Yes, I know what goes on at the GSA. I want our gay kids to feel like there's a place where they belong. Those brochures are not pornographic. They're informational. Gay teens need to know how they can safely explore their sexuality."[3]

It's even in the comic books.

According to the Associated Press (December 10, 2002) the Rawhide Kid, a longtime Marvel Comics cowboy, is "coming out of the closet." He will now dress differently and run with a different crowd.

> A new story line will reveal the Kid's keen fashion sense—including a stylish leather outfit—in what one Marvel editor boasted would be "the first gay Western." . . . In keeping with the light theme, the writer will be Ron Zimmerman, a frequent guest on the Howard Stern radio show and a television writer. . . . The Rawhide character will not walk out of the closet and into a saloon. . . . "He doesn't come out and say he's gay," explained Joe Quesada, editor-in-chief at Marvel. "But it's obvious through his actions and the things he says that his preference is men, not women. . . ."
>
> Among the clues to the Kid's sexuality will include his reaction to other characters from the comic book, including Wild Bill Hickock and the Lone Ranger. "I think that mask and powder-blue outfit are fantastic," he says of the Ranger. "I can certainly see why that Indian follows him around."

Teaching Appreciation for Diversity

In California education officials are advising that there be curricula to "foster appreciation for diversity" and to discourage discriminatory attitudes and practices. California's superintendent of public instruction formed a thirty-six–member advisory task force to translate all of this into state education codes.

While the task force was announced as being a champion of diversity, there was little diversity shown in the orientation of the people who make it up. It was loaded with gay activists and sympathizers affiliated with such fringe groups as Older Asian Sisters in Solidarity (OASIS) and Lavender Youth Recreation and Information Center (LYRIC), as well as more mainstream outfits such as GLSEN and the National Education Association and Gay Caucus.

On April 21, 2001, after laboring for months in closed-door meetings, the task force presented its recommendations in a twenty-one–page report that included the following recommendations:

1. Surveying school children to probe their attitudes about homosexuality.
2. Integrating pro-homosexual and pro-transgender messages into all curricula including science, history, language arts, and even math.
3. Creating new policies "to reduce the adverse impact of gender segregation . . . related to locker room facilities, restrooms and dress."
4. Posting "positive grade level appropriate visual images" that include "all sexual orientations and gender identities" throughout the school.
5. Using taxpayer dollars to establish Gay-Straight Alliances on campuses, put all school personnel through extensive and ongoing sensitivity training, pay for a media blitz, "provide rehabilitation to perpetrators of discrimination and appoint a person in each school to monitor implementation of the new programs."[4]

While children are being taught about the gay lifestyle, there are some things about such a lifestyle that are being suppressed. "Children are never told that homosexual practices lead directly to Hepatitis B infection," writes Stanley Monteith, M.D., "a massive incidence of venereal disease and a compulsive, addictive sexual lifestyle with severe emotional problems. Children are never told of the high suicide rates among homosexuals or the sadness and isolation felt by these tragic people. They are educating our children only about the positive aspects of the homosexual lifestyle in order to encourage the curiosity of youth and lead our young people into the homosexual way of death."[5]

Times and child-rearing practices have drastically changed. All change is not bad, but this change is. CNN recently reported on a "Gayby Boom" to describe the phenomenon of homosexual couples bringing their "children" to homosexual rallies. The days are long gone when children were confronted with male and female role models and when questions of sexual identity were not discussed. Children are now free to pick their gender roles. Christina Hoff Sommers writes:

> Throughout most of human history, children learned about virtue and honor by hearing or reading the inspiring stories of great men and women. By the 1990s this practice, which many educators regarded as too directive, was giving way to practices that suggested to students that they were their own best guides in life. This turn to the autonomous subject as the ultimate moral authority is a notable consequence of the triumph of the progressive style over traditional directive methods of education.[6]

We are no longer teaching our children to admire the virtuous men and women of the past, but are setting before them individuals and groups of questionable morals. Progressive education has turned children loose to explore and develop their own set of values. However, contrary to all statements and appearances, these values are not really their own. Children are simply mimicking what they see in the society around them. How long this can continue before society collapses is anyone's guess.

Parents, Do You Know What Some
Would Like To Do With Your Children?

NAMBLA, the acronym for the North American Man-Boy Love Association, is one of the more vocal organizations pushing for the removal of age-of-consent laws. The organization believes that sex between adults and children—the preferred terminology is "intergenerational relationships"—is perfectly good as long as the child consents. The removal of age-of-consent laws would make sexual relations between adults and consenting children legal.

NAMBLA director David Thorstad says that there is a natural and wholesome attraction to boys that is quite "irrepressible," something like the attraction homosexuals have for each other. On the NAMBLA website Thorstad states: "Pederasty, like homosexuality, has existed, and exists, in all societies that have ever been studied. Homoeroticism is a ubiquitous feature of human experience, as even efforts to repress it confirm. Men and youths have always been attracted to each other, and, like homosexuality in general, their love is irrepressible."

Pederasts want the age of consent laws removed so that they can engage in their sexual proclivities at the taxpayer's expense. Thorstad gives a word of personal testimony.

> In my own case, my boyfriend is now 18, but when he was 16 I could not approach any government or state agencies for assistance with schooling or anything else for fear that moralists and television reporters would turn our life into a living hell. The law stipulates that any person who works in counseling, psychiatry, psychology, social work, teaching and so on, who merely suspects that an illegal sexual relationship may be going on, must report it to the authorities. Investigation, harassment, hysterical and inaccurate publicity, arrest and imprisonment are the likely result.[7]

With the way things are going, Thorstad could see his wishes fulfilled and find that both society and the law is on his side. "Cultural experts who agree with claims that the Supreme Court may have opened the door to legalizing pedophilia in its *Lawrence v. Texas* decision on private homosexual behavior point to the growing movement within academia to destigmatize pedophilia."[8]

While Justice Anthony Kennedy said that the Court's decision "has nothing to do with minors," thinking people may call that statement into question. In a paper entitled "Sex Bias in the U.S. Code," which was prepared for the U.S. Commission on Civil Rights in April 1977, Justice

Ruth Bader Ginsberg advocated lowering the age of consent to twelve years of age.[9]

"The Real Child Abusers"

In 1999, after the book was rejected by several publishers, the University of Minnesota Press published *Harmful to Minors* by Judith Levine. The author argues that traditional sexual standards taught to children by puritanical parents are "harmful to minors." Levine advances the view that there is really no such thing as a pedophile and that such a classification is a myth. This reflects the growing trend to destigmatize pedophilia. During its recent spring meeting the American Psychiatric Association hosted a symposium discussing the removal of pedophilia and other categories of mental illness from its *Diagnostic and Statistical Manual of Mental Disorders* (DSM).

NAMBLA and others of like mind view heterosexual parents, congressmen, and ministers as the real child abusers. In 1994 eighty-two–year–old homosexual activist Harry Hay made the following comments at a press conference in the former Stonewall Inn on Sheridan Square, New York City, site of the riots that launched the modern homosexual movement in June of 1969:

> Insofar as child molestation is concerned, the most common form is the sexual coercion by which gay and lesbian children are bedeviled into hetero identities and behaviors. And this is practiced daily by the whole national and international hetero community—parents, family, teachers, preachers, doctors, lawyers, and Indian chiefs, not to overlook U.S. senators and pooh-bah media. . . .

Did he say "gay and lesbian children"? How does he know? Has anyone ever had their doctor say, "Congratulations, Mrs. Jones. You have just given birth to an eight pound, two ounce homosexual boy"?

Hay continues:

> This outrageous coercion of gay kids into hetero identities and behaviors against their wills is not only sexually abusive, it is spiritually dev-

astating rape, because the child unbecomingly is being led into developing self-loathing at the same time. For this gigantic criminal trespass against not only today's children but against all of us also—all of us—since childhood, from the queers my age of eighty-two down through all the generations of queers assembled here in New York to the gay kids still being bedeviled by sexual coercion against their wills, we the international gay and lesbian people here this week should unite to sue the whole guilty heterosexual community lock, stock, and barrel to within an inch of their lives, and for every nickel they've got, as a beginning of compensation. And while we are at it, we should request our first-class citizenship as well. This could be the class-action suit of the century.[10]

On June 26, 1998, Thorstad spoke to a group of some six hundred people in Mexico City on the history and benefits of pederasty. He stated that

... pederasts believed in an inherent bisexuality of human beings and argued that the influence of the medical profession gave the gay movement the aura of a hospital. Most felt that younger and older males were naturally attracted to each other and that pederasty was a positive good for society because it helped to socialize young males and provided them with a necessary sexual outlet, thereby reducing undesirable social phenomena such as unwanted pregnancies and prostitution.[11]

This kind of reasoning is quite common. Pederasty is viewed as "a positive good for society." The reasons given are highly suspect. Is this the only way, or even a right way, for young men to be "socialized"? Does Thorstad mean to imply that those males who have not engaged in pederasty are not socialized, or poorly socialized? The idea that sexual activity is a method of socialization shows what a beggarly view of humanity such advocates maintain.

Thorstad claims that pederasty reduces "undesirable social phenomena such as unwanted pregnancies and prostitution." Did it ever occur to Thorstad that there are other ways of reducing unwanted pregnancies and prostitution?

Pederasts, however, are convinced that they are right because they have human evolution on their side. One of the NAMBLA articles links their practices to the survival of the species:

> Sir Julian Huxley, the great English biologist, said, at the beginning of this century, no negative trait—and, as you know, a negative trait is one that does not reproduce itself—no negative trait ever appears, and reappears, millennia after millennia after millennia, unless it in some way serves the survival of that species. We gays and lesbians may embody, or have discovered, some things that you folks desperately need to know about.[12]

A negative trait does not reproduce itself. Really? So then, murder, rape, and violence have all reproduced themselves and must therefore be positive traits. The strong taking advantage of the weak, gossip, hatred, maliciousness, disrespect are all plentiful in times past as well as today and, we should expect, will be here tomorrow and the day after, if the Lord tarries. Are all these positive traits?

Homosexuality and Pederasty (Pedophilia)

In the statement by Thorstad in which he claims that the love for men and boys is quite "irrepressible," it will be noted that he compares pederasty with the love that men have for each other—"Men and youths have always been attracted to each other, and, like homosexuality in general, their love is irrepressible." Is there any connection between the two? Are homosexuals frequently found engaging in sex with minors?

The statistics clearly demonstrate that there is an undeniable connection between homosexuality and pedophilia. While there are many more heterosexuals than homosexuals, homosexuals are the major offenders in child sex abuse cases. "In other words, although heterosexuals outnumber homosexuals by a ration of at least 20 to 1, homosexual pedophiles commit about one-third of the total number of child sex offenses."[13]

There is a high likelihood that homosexuals will be homosexual pedophiles. Daily reports that "the evidence shows that homosexual pedophiles cannot be narrowly defined as individuals who are solely attracted to underage boys. In fact, there is considerable overlap between homosexuality and pedophilia."[14]

Though homosexuals often deny this overlap, the evidence is irrefutable. Because there is still a general abhorrence of pedophilia, homosexual activists try to distance the gay lifestyle from pedophilia, yet "there remains a disturbing connection between the two. This is because, by definition, male homosexuals are sexually attracted to other males. While many homosexuals may not seek young sexual partners, the evidence indicates that disproportionate numbers of gay men seek adolescent males or boys as sexual partners."[15]

Studies show that homosexual males are sexually attracted to underage boys. In *The Gay Report,* by homosexual researchers Karla Jay and Allen Young, the authors report data showing that 73 percent of homosexuals surveyed had at some time had sex with boys sixteen to nineteen years of age or younger. Conversely, studies also show that male homosexual pedophiles are sexually attracted to adult males and engage in sexual relations with adult homosexuals.[16]

Homosexual activists claim that they really have the best interests of children at heart. Children, they claim, have sexual rights, too. Allegedly, those of us who oppose pederasty and child pornography are repressive and guilty of stealing the sexual rights of children. According to activists, even child pornography is good for children.

"Legally," writes activist Pat Califa, "young people are not entitled to any kind of sexual expression. The juvenile justice system often deals harshly with young people whose only 'crime' is their homosexuality. Will the anti-pornography movement create a climate in which children can explore their own sexuality with whomever and how ever they choose? . . . Or will it create a more repressive climate in which even less information about sexuality is available and even less sexual variation is tolerated?"[17]

Activists are on a crusade to "help" little children by initiating them.

In its July 1995 issue, the homosexual magazine *Guide* published an editorial and referred to pedophiles as "prophets" of sexual freedom. The editorialist wrote: "We must listen to our prophets. Instead of fearing being labeled pedophiles, we must proudly proclaim that sex includes children's sexuality. . . . Surrounded by pious moralists with deadening anti-sexual rules, we must be shameless trucebreakers, demonstrating our allegiance to a higher concept of love. We must do it for the children's sake."[18]

What do homosexuals really want? They do not simply want the removal of anti-sodomy laws, as occurred in the *Lawrence v. Texas* decision of the U.S. Supreme Court, nor will they rest with the end of so-called discrimination laws against gays. They want age-of-consent laws removed so that pederasty is legal. Congressman William Dannemeyer has stated:

> NAMBLA is a highly visible national organization. . . . They put out a newspaper filled with pictures of male children, they hold conventions, and they appear on network talk shows. Their announced political goal is the elimination or severe alteration of the age-of-consent laws, and they argue their case using the rhetoric of the civil rights movement. Little boys, they say, have as much right as adults to engage in consensual sex, and only a repressive society would prevent them from enjoying such exquisite pleasures at the earliest possible age. One international pedophile has popularized the slogan "Sex before eight, or it's too late."[19]

The Deadly Myth of Consensual Sex with Minors

Pedophiles argue that sex with children is not harmful to children provided that it is consensual. Allegedly, the damage comes from parents and others who overreact or frown on such activities. Parents' prudish views about such matters are "harmful to minors," to use the title of Judith Levine's book. Through such claims pedophiles try to take the blame off of their shoulders for the men and women who have been physically, emotionally, and spiritually damaged by childhood sexual abuse. In a NAMBLA web article entitled "What Does Science Say?" we read:

> The outcomes of sexual experiences between adults and younger people depend on whether the sex was consensual. Also, sexual experiences are powerfully influenced by expectations and the attitudes toward sex which have been passed on to younger people by their parents and social environment. Rigidly anti-sexual attitudes and fears can predispose anyone to harm.... Once sexual experiences have become known by others, secondary harm to youngsters can be induced by the inappropriate reactions of parents, police, social workers, lawyers, and other adults, where no apparent harm results from the sexual contact itself.[20]

But how does one assess consent? Who can tell if a particular child really consents to a sexual encounter with a particular adult in a particular situation? Boys are especially vulnerable because they tell no one how they feel. It's not "manly" to do so. Children are easily manipulated and coerced into silence by an adult frown or word of disapproval. What a lust-driven child predator may consider consent on the part of the child is often nothing more than a fearful silence.

One researcher points out that pedophiles are particularly susceptible to falsely apprehend the child's response and to conclude that it is consensual. "Sex addicts generally need instant gratification. They have a very low threshold for delaying gratification and it's much easier to manipulate a young boy into having sex than it is to manipulate another man."[21]

As we have seen, pedophiles are often homosexuals and homosexuals are often pedophiles. This raises another important issue regarding consent. Because a child may consent to being caressed this does not mean that same child will consent to being sodomized with a bottle. If "intergenerational sex" is permitted, how far will be too far? What kind of activities will be "legal" and which won't? Where does one draw the line?

What might have seemed to be a consensual encounter with a child may later, when that child is grown, be perceived as sexual abuse by that child. The consenting child may, in reality, be a victim of a horrible act.

The Consequences of Homosexual Child Abuse

In a web article entitled "Homosexuality and Child Sexual Abuse" Timothy Dailey cites several studies and writes: "The evidence indicates that a high percentage of homosexuals and pedophiles were themselves sexually abused as children." One study concluded that "boys victimized by older men were over four times more likely to be currently engaged in homosexual activity than were non-victims." Another study concludes: "One of the most salient finds of this study is that 46 percent of homosexual men and 22 percent of homosexual women reported having been molested by a person of the same gender."[22]

Activists are playing with the very souls of children for their own gratification. Many homosexuals have a crazed obsession with youth. Knowing full well that sodomized children practice sodomy, they are pushing hard to create a homosexual world by their assault on children. Here is a promise given a few years ago:

> We shall sodomize your sons, emblems of your feeble masculinity, of your shallow dreams and vulgar lies. We shall seduce them in your schools, in your dormitories, in your gymnasiums, in your locker rooms, in your sports arenas, in your seminaries, in your youth groups, in your movie theater bathrooms, in your army bunkhouses, in your truck stops, in your all-male clubs, in your houses of Congress, wherever men are with men together. Your sons shall become our minions to do our bidding. They will be recast in our image; they will come to crave and adore us.[23]

CHAPTER 3

Destroying the Foundations

If the foundations be destroyed, what can the righteous do?

—Psalm 11:3

We live in a world of change. When the automobile was first introduced it literally changed America, and then the world. The automobile opened a new world of travel and expansion. The suburbs grew as dirt roads were paved and little towns were networked with big cities.

Many other changes have come upon us. In general, because of exponential doubling, science, technology, population growth, the depletion of natural resources, and many other factors are doubling at a faster rate than ever before. My recent book *Suddenly No More Time* [available through Southwest Radio Church Ministries, 1-800-652-1144] details this phenomenon and its prophetic significance.

In and of itself, change is neither moral nor immoral. It is amoral. The automobile came about through an advance in knowledge. It introduced many changes, but the automobile did not destroy the roots and values of society. It may have made certain vices more accessible, but the automobile did not, in itself, endorse or encourage those vices as being good. It did not destroy morality as it was known up to that point and substitute a new set of moral values.

The changes being pushed in every imaginable way by the homosexual community, however, are changing values. The homosexual agenda involves a culture war. It is a war for the minds and souls of men and women, boys and girls. It is aided in its progress by the deterioration of moral values that are a consequences of the erosion of society. If the homosexual agenda is fully implemented it will result in the total paganization of America.

The Spirit of Sodom and the Spirit of Oppression

God warned Israel against engaging in the sexual abominations of the pagan nations through which the people of Israel traveled. "And the LORD spake unto Moses, saying, Speak unto the children of Israel, and say unto them, I am the LORD your God. After the doings of the land of Egypt, wherein ye dwelt, shall ye not do: and after the doings of the land of Canaan, whither I bring you, shall ye not do" (Lev. 18:3).

Why such stern warnings? Was God old-fashioned and narrow-minded? Did He just not realize that the values of one society were just as good as those of any other? Did God need to take a couple of sensitivity classes on being tolerant and open-minded, lest He offend?

Contrary to what twenty-first–century pagans think, God knows what is best. Peace, order, and stability, along with sound mental, emotional, and spiritual health are the results of living in the right way.

Many individuals have purchased a new piece of equipment—maybe a bicycle, lawnmower, or VCR—and have spent literally hours of frustration trying to make it work. As someone once said, "When all else fails, read the instructions." Society is in deep trouble. Will people realize that they have not followed the instructions for the good life?

Leviticus chapters eighteen through twenty list a variety of sexual deviations found in pagan nations. Leviticus 18:21–25 states:

> And thou shalt not let any of thy seed pass through the fire to Molech
> [the god of the Ammonites], neither shalt thou profane the name of thy

God: I am the LORD. Thou shalt not lie with mankind, as with womankind: it is abomination. Neither shalt thou lie with any beast to defile
thyself therewith: neither shall any woman stand before a beast to lie
down thereto: it is confusion. Defile not ye yourselves in any of these
things: for in all these the nations are defiled which I cast out before
you: And the land is defiled: therefore I do visit the iniquity thereof
upon it, and the land itself vomited out her inhabitants.

These prohibited practices are labeled "abomination" and "confusion"
and are associated with Molech, a false god. Even the land is defiled by
these detestable practices and receives judgment— "And the land is defiled: therefore I do visit the iniquity thereof *upon it.*" False religion and
detestable sexual practices always destroy nations and their people.

In 1893 the World Parliament of Religions was held in Chicago, Illinois. Religious leaders from all over the world came because they believed that all religions are basically the same and that "we are all working together as brothers and sisters and that we are all going to the same
place." It was truly a world ecumenical movement and set the stage for
the rising ecumenism that made so many advances in the twentieth century.

A group of Bible-believing Presbyterian missionaries, however, realized that we are not all working together as brothers and sisters and that
we are not all going to the same place. Moreover, they realized that pagan religions would lead to pagan practices and to the accompanying
vices. These missionaries published a statement that was true at the end
of the nineteenth century and is still true in the twenty-first:

Just as Buddha, Mohammed, Confucius, Krishna, and Zoroaster remain
to this day decayed by irrevocable death, so the religions that bear their
names carry with them the stench of the grave. *Poverty, barbarity, death,
and lasciviousness must be the lot of those men and nations that follow after
them.* The horrors of children left to die, women sacrificed to dumb
idols, *families destroyed by fleshly perversion,* and the sick given over to
their own devices are the fruit of the flesh that no heathen ravings can

be rid. Only the Gospel of our Savior Jesus Christ, the Way, the Truth, and the Life, can lend the bequest of life. Only Christ has Himself escaped the shackles of death, and only the faith in Him that comes through grace *can free men from the oppressions of the spirit of Sodom, which we must affirm is the same as your precious spirit of cooperation, toleration, and empathy.*[1]

The same evils which these missionaries spoke about more than a century ago are the evils that are cropping up in America. The spirit of Molech wields the abortionists knife and families are "destroyed by fleshly perversion." "The oppressions of the spirit of Sodom" are now being seen in enforced speech codes and politically-correct legislation that is making certain portions of the Bible illegal.

Homosexuals pursue their perversion with an animal-like ferocity and some seek additional thrills by inflicting pain. The use of spiked collars and whips and other paraphernalia often produces injuries which require medical attention. Some even torture their sex partners with needles, razors, and tongs. In addition to such sadomasochistic antics, "many homosexuals also indulge in bestiality, that is to say, sex with animals." Some even include animals in their lists of fantasies. Because of the variety of sexual expressions exhibited, homosexual behavior could be called "pansexual" or "omnisexual."[2]

What will happen to a society where perversion is encouraged and the characters viewed on TV at prime time endorse such practices? Should the TV show "Queer Eye for a Straight Guy" be renamed "Devilish Fantasies for a Dying Nation"?

America is looking more like Canaan. Could it be that the reason America is not specifically mentioned in Bible prophecy is because when the end-time events begin to unfold we will have ceased to exist as a nation?

"Is This Marriage?"
The home and family is the central pillar of civilization. The pillar, however, is being torn down.

Why should a state grant a marriage license to a same-sex couple? There can be no other reason than "they have requested it." But why have they requested it? What could be their possible motivation? If it is because they are "friends," then we have to ask: "Do friends need a marriage certificate, or license, to live together?"

Make no doubt about it, homosexuality is not about friendships. It is about granting certain rights and privileges that often involve tax breaks and financial advantages to people who engage in same-sex activities. Jan LaRue, chief counsel for Concerned Women for America, writes: "Granting a marriage license to homosexuals because they engage in sex is as illogical as granting a medical license to a barber because he wears a white coat or a law license to a salesman because he carries a briefcase. Real doctors, lawyers, and the public would suffer as a result of licensing the unqualified and granting them rights, benefits, and responsibilities as if they were qualified."[3]

Allowing two people of the same sex to "marry" will devalue marriage. A license for homosexual "marriage" means that the government recognizes that particular relationship as being legitimate and equal to the relationship of one man and one woman. Any time a lesser thing is made equal to a greater thing, the greater thing is devalued. "If the Smithsonian Museum displays a hunk of polished blue glass next to the Hope Diamond with a sign that says, 'These are of equal value, and treats them as if they were, the Hope Diamond is devalued in the public's eye."[4]

Evidently, the idea of same-sex "marriages" has been catching on. We are now seeing same-sex couples at high school proms.

A Southwest Radio Church Ministries *Bible in the News* report for July 9, 2003, relates how more gay teenagers than ever before are taking same-sex dates to the prom. Instead of being shocked, schools are saying, "So what's the big deal?" The MSNBC report cited stated that "it has become almost commonplace in urban and suburban areas for a student to bring a date of the same sex to the prom—and that in most schools, it's really no big deal."

All of this is a reflection of the significant shift in the last few decades of how society has come to view lesbians and gays. In contrast to the past decades—when images of homosexuals were coarse or nonexistent—today people with alternate sexual orientations appear everywhere from MTV to the wedding page of the *New York Times*. Gay young people are less reluctant to identify themselves as such and some even view it as a sign of cultural sophistication.

The above-cited report states that because of this growing acceptability of homosexuality, young people are identifying themselves as "gay" at younger ages than ever before. In the 1970s it was the mid-twenties, but today it's sixteen for boys and seventeen for girls. This is partly due to the fact that high school clubs that promote awareness of gay issues—and which also offer gay and bisexual teens a safe place to express themselves—are increasing in number throughout America.

With the gay lifestyle becoming more acceptable, school administrators generally agree that there's no reason why kids shouldn't announce their sexual orientation. "I went to the administration and asked if it was all right if I wore a tuxedo and went to prom with a girl," said one teenage girl in Colorado. "They said, 'All right, sure'. . . . It was kind of funny . . . when we first got to prom my date Ashley and I had to go to the bathroom. When I walked in there, everybody stopped putting on their makeup and looked at me strange. Then I told them, 'It's all right, I'm a girl too.'"

Many adults and teenagers feel that same-sex "marriages" are "fair" and appeal to the argument of justice and equality. This argument states that society should allow homosexual marriages because homosexuals should be entitled to the same rights, privileges, and benefits that heterosexuals receive. Why should one be favored above the other? Homosexuals are particularly vociferous in arguing the point. Same-sex "marriages" would provide certain financial benefits. Someone once said, "If you can't figure out why, follow the money trail." From tax breaks to insurance coverage, society generally bestows a variety of financial incentives on those who "tie the knot," so to speak. While the claim is that it is all about fairness, equality, and accommodating the "legitimate" sexual needs of the gay community, there's more to it than that. Ed Vitagliano says this argument is like an onion, with one principle layered on top of another. Once you begin to peel away the layers your eyes begin to burn.[5]

The egalitarian argument proves too much, however. If it is allowed and you begin to peel off layers all kinds of noxious effects follow. Who, for example, is to say that marriage to animals should not be lawful, sanctioned, and financed by the state? If sexual arrangements are valid, provided that they are motivated by "love," then why can't someone say they love their dog and want to "marry" Fido? When state and society admit that traditional marriage is only one of many possible options, the possibilities are without number. Where, then, does one draw the line without being arbitrary and seemingly close-minded to the possibilities? Dailey's observations are noteworthy:

> There is little evidence that homosexuals as a whole desire to "settle down" to conventional marriage. Gay activists have made it abundantly clear that they have no intention of imitating the restrictive morality of "breeders," their contemptuous designation for parents.
>
> Romance between a man and a woman naturally blossoms into marriage, children, and the building of society. That's God's wonderful and fulfilling design for human sexuality. Homosexual infatuation can accomplish none of those goals, but can only culminate in hollow, unnatural lust. Hence the relentless drive for the next "conquest" in a vain attempt to find meaning in the sexual act.[6]

"Doesn't Marriage Have Something To Do with Producing Children?"

It is impossible to discuss marriage and sexuality without giving some place in the scheme of things to bearing children. And it is also true that only two people—one man and one woman—can produce children. This means that marriage between one man and one woman is rooted in the nature of things. When the state recognizes marriage between one man and one woman it is simply giving recognition to a natural order that has always existed. This is the natural basis for marriage and undergirds the apostle's words when he writes, "for even their women did change the natural use into that which is against nature: And likewise also the men, leaving the natural use of the woman" (Rom. 1:26–27).

That marriage was intended to produce children, however, often draws heated protests from those who advocate same-sex "marriages." "What about a man and a woman who decide not to have children, or what about a man and a woman who cannot have children? Does this mean that they cannot marry?" They will also throw in the argument of the lesbian couple who decides to raise children through artificial insemination. If children are the goal of marriage then two lesbians can have their own children in artificial ways. Does this mean that lesbians can "procreate" and therefore be allowed to marry?

If a man and a woman decide to marry and not have children, that says nothing about the intent of marriage, but only about their intent for *their* marriage. The infertile couple likewise demonstrates the procreative connection to marriage, for infertile couples often undergo medical procedures that remedy the cause of the infertility. These are exceptional cases but the exception proves the rule. The lesbian who decides to be artificially inseminated likewise does not demonstrate that marriage and procreation are unrelated. In fact just the opposite is demonstrated. The lesbian cannot have a child apart from a sperm donor.

Yet same-sex advocates continue to press their point by saying that marriage is not about procreation. It is about love and commitment. But should love and commitment to animals be considered marriage? A golfer may love his golf clubs but should that person be allowed to marry his golf clubs and receive survivor benefits if something happens to them? And can't a man "love" two men? Why limit "marriage" between two men, or two women. How about gay polygamous relationships? Harvard law professor Martha L. Minow favors same-sex "marriage" but she hasn't made up her mind about polygamy. "Too bad," writes Vitagliano. "She has thrown open the door for her cat, but is not sure whether or not she would like snakes, spiders and rats to come in through the same door."[7]

Same-Sex "Families"

Homosexual advocates contend that same-sex "families" are just like other families. Children with two mommies, or with two daddies, adjust quite well and grow up to be wholesome, well-rounded individuals.

As we are going to see in chapter seven, many homosexuals claim that they are good Christian people who are following the Bible. They argue that the Bible does not really condemn homosexual relationships, but only abusive homosexual relationships.

For those gays who claim that they are following the Bible, however, the concept of same-sex "families" presents a major problem. Whenever the Bible speaks about families it speaks about a mother, a father, and children. You will hunt in vain to find a same-sex family in the Bible. Though same-sex relations are mentioned in Scripture, they are always condemned. Homosexual and lesbian relationships are never presented in Scripture as "family relationships." Those who are seeking to create same-sex "families" are changing the natural order. This is the offense of Romans 1—they "changed the glory of the incorruptible God into an image" (vs. 23), "who changed the truth of God into a lie" (vs. 25), "for even their women *did change* the natural use into that which is against nature" (vs. 26). Homosexual relationships and homosexual "families" represent man's arrogant attempt to change what must not be changed.

In Genesis 2:24–25 we read: "Therefore shall a man leave his father and mother, and shall cleave to his wife: and they shall be one flesh. And they were both [Adam and Eve] naked, the man and his wife, and were not ashamed."

This text speaks of a man and his wife. Normally the man has a father and mother. The man's responsibility is to cleave to his wife. This is the Edenic pattern, but it is also the pattern for all of society. Adam did not have a father and mother, but was made by God. The mention of a man leaving his father and mother suggests that this is God's design for succeeding generations.

Polls suggest that many Americans are now coming to view the idea of same-sex "marriages" and "families" with greater acceptance. Of those polled at the end of June 2003, 55 percent said that homosexual "marriages" should not be given official recognition by the state. When the same question was asked in 1996, however, 68 percent said that homosexual "marriages" should be given government recognition. Obviously, some people are changing their minds. But do they know the whole story?

Gay households often produce children with problems. Children who have been raised in homosexual households show a much greater likelihood of engaging in sexual experimentation. In an age of STDs and HIV this can be highly dangerous.

Recent studies indicate that 0.3 percent of adult females surveyed report having engaged in homosexual acts in the last year, 0.4 percent in the last five, and 3 percent have engaged in homosexual acts in their lifetimes. However, 12 percent of the children of lesbians become active lesbians, which is a much higher incidence than that of the general adult female population.

The same contrast is seen in the adult male population. While almost 5 percent of males report having engaged in homosexual sex sometime during their lifetimes, the number of homosexuals who practice exclusive homosexual sex is much less, between 1 and 2 percent. However, one study found that 9 percent of the adult sons of homosexual fathers were homosexual in their adult lives.[8]

The rate of incest in homosexual homes is also much higher than in non-homosexual homes. One study found that "a disproportionate percentage—29 percent—of the adult children of homosexual parents had been specifically subjected to sexual molestation by that homosexual parent, compared with only 0.6 percent of adult children of heterosexual parents having reported sexual relations with their parent. . . . Having a homosexual parent(s) appears to increase the risk of incest with a parent by a factor of about 50."[9]

While gays often talk about the danger they are in from so-called "hate crimes" against them committed by heterosexuals, the facts show that they are in much greater danger from their homosexual partner. As many as 650,000 gay men appear to be victims of domestic violence each year in the United States, and lesbian violence is about equal. Gay Glenn, president of the American Family Association in Michigan, argues that if mainstream media wanted to be effective rather than politically correct, the media would "shine the light on the semi-secret of homosexual violence against one another."[10]

There are, therefore, many reasons—both biblical and otherwise—to oppose homosexual "marriages" and homosexual "families." Many politicians, however, are not interested in logic or sanity, but want to win votes, no matter where they come from. Some presidential candidates and others who are courting votes try to straddle the fence somewhat and still win votes from the gay community by promising to support "gay unions." John Kerry, for example, says that he supports a federal law enacting homosexual civil unions, but is opposed to homosexual "marriage" because of how he views the world "culturally, historically, and religiously." He believes, however, that "civil unions would grant homosexuals all the rights of marriage."[11]

The New Gay Rights Advocate—The U.S. Supreme Court

Five years ago, in a Houston apartment, Tyron Garner and John Geddes Lawrence were arrested by police officers who were enforcing a Texas anti-sodomy law, and fined two hundred dollars for performing a homosexual act. By a 6-3 decision the highest court in the land struck down the Texas law and opened the door to unbelievably radical and wide sweeping changes in the way America understands and treats a variety of moral issues. David Garrow, legal scholar at Emory University and Pulitzer prize-winning biographer of Martin Luther King, Jr., said the *Lawrence* case is "the most libertarian majority opinion ever issued by the Supreme Court. It's arguably bigger than *Roe v. Wade*."[12]

This Supreme Court decision to strike down the Texas anti-sodomy law shows that the Supreme Court has now become an active participant in the culture war and is using its might to move victory in a certain preconceived direction. Justice Antonin Scalia put it bluntly when he said, "It is clear . . . that the Court has taken sides in the culture war, departing from its role of assuring, as neutral observer, that the democratic rules of engagement are observed."[13]

Obviously, the Supreme Court views itself as an agent of social and moral change and, by virtue of its legal power, has the ability to impose its own morality on the nation. Many legal experts agree that this is a new, and unconstitutional development. "The *Lawrence* decision illustrates that a solid majority of the Supreme Court has overstepped its constitutional authority and now sees itself as essentially a dictatorial body. By decree the Court can abolish any state law provoking its disfavor or obstructing its desired course of social revolution."[14]

The Effects of the Decision on the Gay Community

The Court's decision was welcomed by gays around America. Following the decision photos flashed in the media of large crowds of people carrying signs "We Won!" interspersed with pictures of men holding hands, others in passionate embrace—men lip to lip with men, women lip to lip with women—were displayed on magazine covers and on the front page of newspapers as gays celebrated the decision.

On Sunday, June 29, 2003, just a few days after the *Lawrence* decision was made public, hundreds of thousands of people were reported taking to the streets for Gay Pride parades across America. Fox News reported:

> The events in cities around the country maintained their colorful, Carnival-like atmosphere. They featured naked cyclists, fluffy pink boas and floats swaying with singing drag queens. As in years past, the lesbian motorcycle group Dykes on Bikes got the San Francisco parade off to a roaring start with hundreds of leather-clad and topless women astride motorcycles.[15]

Geoffrey Kors, director of Equality California stated: ""The symbolism of the nation's highest court recognizing the validity of gay relationships is just really important for the community because it shows we live in a society where we can create change with laws, not violence." Reporter Lisa Leff commented, "The high court's 6-3 decision overturned not only the Texas statute but apparently swept away laws in a dozen other states that ban oral and anal sex for everyone, or for homosexuals in particular."[16]

The Effects of the Decision on Morality and Legislation

The *Lawrence* decision has encouraged the acceptance of other forms of deviant sexual behaviors and has granted them a degree of respectability. Cultural experts agree that the decision has opened the door to legalizing pedophilia, something that is not far in the future.[17] The Court, which was generally cautious in its views, has now teamed up with those who are not cautious and who put a premium on violating accepted values.

Thanks to the Supreme Court, it will be harder to rule against almost any kind of sexual activity. In fact, an Ohio attorney who specializes in defending the distribution of sex magazines, has moved to overturn Ohio's obscenity law on the basis of the *Lawrence* decision. Attorney H. Louis Sirkin told Common Pleas Judge Richard A. Niehaus in Cincinnati that "practically all choices made by consenting adults regarding their own sexual practices are a matter of personal liberty and thus beyond the reach of state control."

Citing what legal experts call a "due process right to privacy," Sirkin noted the recent Supreme Court references "to bedrooms and sanctity of the home in the sodomy decision and other rulings—including on abortion, contraception, and parental rights." Sirkin's statements were made in connection with the arrest of Mr. Shawn Jenkins who was arrested in October of 2001. Jenkins faces up to a year in prison on one count of pandering obscenity at his Tip Top Magazines store. The *Washington Times* report states that "the suit is among the first to reach beyond homosexual issues in using the high court's June 26 decision baring states from criminalizing 'sexual practices common to a homosexual lifestyle.'" Sirkin is known for getting a Ohio court to strike down the Child Pornography Prevention Act of 1996.[18]

The Court and the Constitution

The Supreme Court has made a vicious attack on the U.S. Constitution and the basic principles of American law and government. In its professed desire to create equality for all sexual orientations it has introduced the concept of "rights" as understood by the Socialist left. "Rights are social entitlements that can be created by the government." This is not the position of the American founders and has no affinity with the American Revolution, but can be traced rather to the French Revolution. "Both the Declaration of Independence and the Constitution regard entitlements as endowments, not of human governments, but of a Divine Creator."[19]

The right to "life, liberty, and the pursuit of happiness" is not something that comes from the government, nor can they be removed by governmental agencies because they are "inalienable." American law and government is based on the presupposition that God is above the government and that the people of the land need to be protected from the government. Hence the Bill of Rights is stated in negative terms—"Congress shall make no law . . ."

How then can the left make this unconscionable assault on the Constitution and use it to support its agenda? By the left's view of the Constitution as a "living" document which can be molded to fit their Socialist schemes. While the founders would have abhorred this emasculating of the Constitution, "the manufacture of rights has become a cottage industry of Democratic legislators and the judges they appoint, and is a principal battle ground of the culture war."[20]

Under the expert leadership of the left, government has moved to the position of deity. Gay rights, the alleged rights of gays to serve in the military, the alleged rights for same-sex couples to marry, are all manufactured rights by those who have ascribed paternal lordship to big government.

The *Lawrence* decision is an act of legislation. It legislates pro-gay morality by striking down a state's laws against sodomy. Richard Marmon, an attorney and friend of Southwest Radio Church Ministries, has said: "It's not whether or not morality will be legislated , but rather whose morality will be legislated." In this case the morality of the liberal left has been imposed on the will of the people. While the Court supported its decision by the claim that it was supporting individual liberties and privacy, the decision was really a blow against liberty. By striking down powers guaranteed to the states, the Court "abetted the growth of the federal leviathan; by cutting down state laws regulating morals in the name of fighting oppression," and launched "federal assaults on individual liberties."[21]

This is certainly not what the founders intended for the Supreme Court. "That sodomy is an inalienable right would no doubt come as a big surprise to the Constitution's framers. They are, of course, the last constitutional experts the Supreme Court would ever consult. The Supreme Court, judging from the majority opinion's slavish attention to Europe's regard for sodomy, is much more interested in the thoughts of modern Danes than dead Americans."[22]

The Court's Decision and Appeal to European Precedent

The justices who were in the *Lawrence* majority made reference to the European Court of Human Rights which addressed a similar case in 2001 with many parallels to the *Lawrence* case. That court held that anti–sodomy laws were not valid under the European Convention on Human Rights. The majority justices also cited a brief filed by former U.N. Human Rights Commissioner Mary Robinson to validate the claim that there is an international consensus supporting "the protected right of homosexual adults to engage in intimate, consensual conduct."[23]

In his dissenting opinion Justice Scalia was quick to express the view that European precedents should have no effect on Supreme Court decisions. Yet that such precedents were given some weight in the High Court's deliberation's demonstrates "an ongoing effort to harmonize our judiciary with the unfolding, U.N.-dominated system of international law."[24]

In 1998 three Supreme Court justices—Sandra Day O'Connor, Stephen Breyer, and Ruth Bader Ginsberg—were among a delegation of American judges who took a European tour. The purpose of the tour was to begin the process of internationalizing U.S. laws by integrating European judicial precedents into U.S. court decisions. Justice O'Connor stated: "In the next century, we are going to want to draw upon judgments from other jurisdictions. . . . We are going to be more inclined to look at the decisions of [the European] court . . . and perhaps use them and cite them . . . we are going to see in the next century a considerable amount of litigation coming out of [international] treaties."[25]

This was another blow against American law and government in the *Lawrence* decision. The tragedy of this is that our nation's moral and legal foundations are diametrically at variance with those of modern Europe. The Declaration of Independence, which would be struck down by the European Court of Human Rights, states that "all men are created equal, that they are endowed by their Creator with certain unalienable Rights." According to one of America's most venerable documents, this means that there is an authority higher than government to which government is morally accountable—something that the European system now denies. The only reason the liberal left is citing European precedent is because it favors the leanings of the left.

According to Alan E. Sears, president of the Alliance Defense Fund, "In *Lawrence*, the court announced a new, fabricated constitutional right to engage in sodomy. Its arguments were so questionable that the majority in *Lawrence* had to refer not just to the legal alchemy of *Griswold v. Connecticut* in its construct of the right to privacy, but felt compelled to appeal to European courts to justify the desired conclusion." Sears notes that "with such an appeal to European precedent, the court may have laid the groundwork for far more mischief down the road than most recognize."[26]

It Wasn't Always This Way

In 1986 the U.S. Supreme Court upheld the anti-sodomy laws of the state of Georgia in the *Bowers* decision. But how could the Supreme Court give a ruling completely opposite one it gave just seventeen years earlier? Was it in error when it upheld the Georgia law?

Not at all. The answer has something to do with a new view of right and wrong. The recent Supreme Court decision argues that the earlier *Bowers* decision was incompatible with "an emerging awareness that liberty gives substantial protection to adult persons in deciding how to conduct their private lives in matters pertaining to sex."[27] Rather than basing decisions on ultimate views of right and wrong, the Supreme Court is now saying that the individual is the final and highest law in these matters.

The ease with which the Supreme Court reversed its position on anti-sodomy laws in June of 2003 ought to be a wake-up call to everyone. Seventeen years prior to the recent *Lawrence* decision which overturned the earlier *Bowers* decision, Chief Justice Warren Burger said this about his 1986 concurring majority in *Bowers*:

> Decisions of individuals relating to homosexual conduct have been subject to state intervention throughout the history of Western Civilization. Condemnation of those practices is firmly rooted in Judeo-Christian moral and ethical standards. . . . [Sir William] Blackstone described "the infamous crime against nature" as an offense of "deeper malignity" than rape, a heinous act "the very mention of which is a disgrace to human nature" and "a crime not fit to be named." To hold that the act of homosexual sodomy is somehow protected as a fundamental right would be to cast aside millennia of moral teaching.[28]

The highest Court of the land has consistently held—until very recently—that the state does have a compelling interest in criminalizing certain kinds of destructive behaviors. Scott Lively, director of the Pro-Family Law Center in Sacramento, California, which filed a brief supporting the Texas anti-sodomy law, stated: "If the state doesn't have even a legitimate interest in criminalizing sodomy . . . how can the state continue to regulate against group sexual encounters, sadomasochism, sex between brothers and sisters, sex with animals and sex with corpses?"[29]

CHAPTER 4

Laws That Silence

... and causeth the earth and them which dwell therein to worship the first beast.

—Revelation 13:12

An analysis of the homosexual movement shows that it has implemented two strategies that are imposed simultaneously. One is to disseminate their views in whatever way possible. The other strategy involves silencing those who are opposed to their agenda. Every fascist movement has proceeded in the same way. Indeed, it is right to say that when we look at the homosexual agenda we are seeing "homofascism" at work.

One only has to look at Hitler's Germany, Stalin's Russia, Castro's Cuba, along with a host of others to realize the similarities. There have been "the brown shirts," "the black shirts," and now "the pink shirts." Homosexuals have distinctive hair styles and styles of dress. While it is not quite accurate to say that there is a "homosexual uniform," there is a uniformity of style and dress that identifies who they are and what they stand for.

Though some may think the term "homofascism" is unkind and

overdrawn, let's look at how the gays are seeking to stifle all speech and religious expression that is contrary to the gay agenda and how it is seeking to block all opposition.

1. The Bible is to be condemned because it allegedly promotes hostility and even violence against gays.
2. Certain kinds of sermons are to be banned and the pastors preaching those forbidden sermons are to be fined, their churches could be pressured by being threatened with the loss of tax exemptions, and members of their congregations harassed.
3. Telling a homosexual "Jesus can change you" is to be made a criminal offense. It implies that Jesus doesn't love them the way they are and that they are inferior to those who are heterosexual.
4. Clergy must participate in "gay marriages" and can be fined and/or incarcerated if they refuse.
5. Parents who object to courses in school that endorse homoeroticism or that present it as normal, or who want their children to opt out of such courses are to be fined and to be regarded as having committed an act of child abuse against their children.
6. Churches must hire homosexual pianists, organists, and nursery workers.
7. Churches are to be forbidden from firing a staff person who "comes out" and declares he or she is gay.
8. It will be illegal to teach that certain kinds of diseases are characteristic of the homosexual lifestyle.
9. It will be illegal to express the opinion that one does not favor homosexual dental hygienists, nurses, and doctors because of the possibility of infecting patients with HIV.
10. It will be illegal to challenge the claim advanced by many homosexuals that homosexuality is valid because animals in the wild are known to engage in homosexual relations.

Farfetched? I will let the reader be the judge. But before coming to a conclusion, read on.

The Thought Police Are Watching

In 1990 President Bush signed the "Hate Crimes Statistics Act" in the presence of twenty homosexual rights activists who had been invited to the White House for the occasion. This law set the precedent for a new brand of favors and helps to homosexuals. It authorized the U.S. Attorney General to collect data on a special kind of criminal act—crimes that grow out of prejudice based on race, religion, sexual orientation, ethnicity, or any other category that may be deemed appropriate.

Of course, it was *already* illegal to perform acts of violence against individuals irrespective of their race, religion, sexual orientation, and so on. Beating up on a person no matter what their ethnicity or views has never been a legally protected act. This new legislation, however, went beyond acts of violence to what are ostensibly wrong opinions. Hate crimes legislation and enforced speech codes turn government officials into "thought police." What does this mean and how will it affect religious liberties?

Supposedly, Americans have the constitutional freedom to hold opinions—even if those opinions are immoral, antisocial, or subversive to the government. Though there have been unfortunate exceptions to this tradition of liberty from time to time, it is, nonetheless, a vital part of the American legal heritage. But now, homosexuals wish to end this legacy. Permanently. They want the state to punish people for holding "wrong" opinions.[1]

Hate Crimes Legislation

The United States Department of Justice defines hate crimes as crimes motivated by a "negative bias against persons, property, or organizations based solely on race, religion, ethnicity/national origin, sexual orientation, or disability." If an individual is a victim of a crime primarily because of any of these characteristics, the crime is then considered to be motivated by hate.[2]

Though the concept of hate crimes seems to be a good thing, it actually creates "classes" of victims. Depending on the class to which the victim belongs, the crime is considered to have differing degrees of severity and therefore warrants differing degrees of punishment. Can we avoid the conclusion that this is a kind of reverse discrimination? Isn't it wrong for a victim to have more, or less, protection because of the class to which that individual belongs? How does the concept of "equal justice for all" fit in with hate crimes? It doesn't seem to fit at all. If you are a person of color who kisses salamanders on the lips and you live with a person of the same gender, stealing your wallet could be a very serious offense!

Imagine the following scenarios.

One day Bill is walking down the street near his apartment and is robbed and beaten. That same afternoon John is walking down the street near his apartment and is also robbed and beaten. These are both crimes that are punishable by law. Under hate crimes laws, however, if it can be shown that John was robbed and beaten because of his affiliation with a certain group, the person who robbed and beat John could find that federal officials are being used to investigate and prosecute his case, while Bill's case would be handled by local authorities. Though Bill may have been just as injured and traumatized as John, Bill may find that because of local inefficiency or lack of funds, or because the criminal knows "the right people," his attacker may ultimately go free. John, however, may find that the government is actually providing him with legal assistance. He may even have government-appointed bodyguards protecting him in the event that he is threatened by the family and friends of the attacker. This means that every citizen does not have equal protection under the law. White heterosexuals who are conservative Christians and in good health may have to kiss justice under the law goodbye.

This is not an overstatement. While heterosexuals are to refrain from making derogatory statements against gays that could incite acts of hatred against them, this evidently does not apply to pro-gay groups and individuals.

For example, some of the diversity seminars clearly raise animosity against Christians and others who believe that the homosexual lifestyle presents unique problems of health and morality to society. David French, Christian attorney and author of *A Season for Justice,* writes:

> I had the privilege of viewing a popular diversity presentation that began by showing a picture of the "new face of discrimination in America." The presenter flashed a slide of a handsome young man. With his voice quivering, he said, "This is my son, and he is gay." He then commenced a sixty-minute impassioned diatribe against "heterosexism," saying that true nondiscrimination means acceptance, tolerance, and understanding. The speech was laced with implicit and explicit insults of religious views that condemned homosexual behavior.[3]

What Sexual Orientation Has To Do with Legislation

Homosexuals are working to get sexual orientation included in hate crimes legislation. Once that is accomplished they will have law enforcement on their side. The full force of the law will then be brought against people who oppose homosexuality. Not a single Christian group, or any other group that opposes homosexuality, will be left unaffected. Christians will not be able to voice their convictions, or to act on their convictions. How will this play out?

Recently, a California court found two Christian doctors in San Diego county to be in error when they refused to artificially inseminate a lesbian who, allegedly, was "traumatized by the discrimination." In the Netherlands, Dutch authorities almost prosecuted Pope John Paul II because he said that a homosexual advocacy march was "an offense to Christian values."[4] Is it not a harbinger of things to come that homosexual activists who make their cases on the basis of liberty want to curtail everyone else's liberties?

Make no doubt about it, homosexuals are not adverse to filing lawsuits even against those who would object to homosexuals showing affection for each other in the public workplace. A case in point is a Swedish company that was forced to pay a former employee approximately $6,800 in damages after the employee accused her boss of homophobia for expressing his displeasure over a public lesbian kiss the employee shared with her girl friend.[5] And it's happening in America, too, as the following indicates.

Prior to his firing in October, Rolf Szabo had worked for Eastman Kodak for 23 years. By all accounts Szabo, a resident of Greece, New York, was a capable and conscientious employee. But Szabo discovered that under the new workplace dogma of "diversity" job performance is less important than displaying correct attitudes. In early October, according to Rochester ABC television affiliate WOKR, Kodak's diversity group sent out an e-mail asking employees to "be supportive" of colleagues who choose to come out on Gay and Lesbian Coming-Out Day.

Replying to the message, Szabo tersely told Kodak's sensitivity commissars to stop sending him e-mails that he considered "disgusting and offensive." "I don't need this to do my job," Szabo explained. "It has nothing to do with gay issues. It could have been any other topic. It's just that enough is enough. We really don't need this to do our jobs."

According to Szabo, Kodak officials demanded that he sign a letter renouncing his "homophobic" attitudes. When he refused he was fired. "The Eastman Kodak Company gives me a paycheck; they don't own me," Szabo told WOKR. "I'll go somewhere else for a paycheck, that's all."[6]

Why is all of this happening now? Is it some chance phenomena, a fortuitous happening of random events, or is there more involved than meets the eye?

In their book *The Homosexual Agenda: Exposing the Principal Threat to Religious Freedom Today*, Alan Sears and Craig Osten remind us that this is part of an international conspiracy working at home and abroad, at the grass roots and in legislatures, to reform society. It is seeking to use all of the legal means possible to silence all opposition. They report:

On June 25, 2001, Judy Guerin of the National Coalition for Sexual Freedom gave a speech at the fifteenth annual World Congress of Sexology in Paris. Her speech discussed her organization's plan to reform sexual laws in the United States. Her talk outlined the agenda of radical homosexual activists and their allies to push their agenda through federal, state, and local legislatures and bring the full weight of government pressure and laws down on those who hold biblical standards of sexual behavior.[7]

Much of this has already been underway for several years. The "teeth" of this monster are the anti-discrimination laws that are being placed on the books in various locales. In 2001, for example, Governor Gray Davis of California signed AB-1475 which cleverly removed the religious exemption that allowed religious organizations to "discriminate" against gays in hiring and firing policies because of religious convictions. The religious exemption also sheltered Baptist and Catholic hospitals from anti-discrimination laws that included sexual orientation. However, if the hospital accepts patients who are not of the hospital's persuasion and religion the hospital is immediately subject to anti-discrimination laws that include sexual orientation.

Davis also signed SB-225 which mandated that private schools, many of which are religious and believe that homosexuality is out of the perfect will of God, adopt non-discrimination policies supporting sexual orientation or face the possibility of being removed from the California Interscholastic Federation and other interscholastic sports programs. This means that both public and private schools must have a non–discrimination policy regarding sexual orientation or they can no longer compete in interscholastic sports.[8]

Religious Harassment

While every Christian has a mandate to share the Gospel of salvation with others it is now considered religious harassment to do so in certain areas.

The Maryland State Board of Education recently approved a new regulation that protects homosexuals from verbal harassment. Under the new rule, students who call each other names or joke about a person's sexual preference face suspension. This could have far-reaching ramifications. If, for example, one student tells a gay student about his faith in Jesus Christ, the gay student could say, "Stop it. You are harassing me. I'm going to complain to the principal about this." A Christian student could find himself facing a legal battle just because he testified to his Savior.[9]

In his book *A Season for Justice,* Christian attorney David French cites the increasing number of religious harassment suits.

- A court in Pennsylvania held that religious statements in the company newsletter and Bible verses printed on company checks were religious harassment.
- The Oregon Unemployment Commissioner ruled that it is religious harassment to permit a Seventh-Day Adventist employee to discuss his religion in the office.
- The state of Oregon also claims that it is religious harassment for a manager to tell an employee that some of his personal habits are immoral.
- A county government in Iowa instructed an employee to refrain from any activity that "could be construed as religious proselytizing, witnessing or counseling" and instructed him to remove from his office all items having a religious connotation, including a desk Bible.
- A division of the California Department of Education bans employees from engaging in any religious discussions in the workplace and prohibits the display or promotion of any religious materials outside the workplace.
- A federal court issued an injunction barring the defendant and any of his employees from making any religious remarks contrary to their fellow employees' religious beliefs.[10]

But who is harassing whom? The Boy Scouts of America have faced criticism because of their position on homosexuality which the politically-correct crowd has labeled "incompatible with anti-discrimination laws."

The Scouts have been barred from public facilities. Individual Scouts have been harassed at public meetings, as when they were booed at the 2000 National Democratic Convention while presenting the colors.[11]

When the New Jersey Supreme Court ruled that the Scouts would have to admit homosexual scout masters, the Boy Scouts appealed to the U.S. Supreme Court which, in a close 5-4 decision, ruled that the Boy Scouts were not subject to New Jersey's laws because the Scouts were a private organization and were at liberty to bar individuals from leadership whose lifestyle was incompatible with the organization's beliefs.

Even after this narrow victory the Scouts were still subjected to continuing harassment. The Scouts' victory only infuriated those who were unhappy with the decision. Pro-gay city and country governments threatened to, and in some cases actually did, prevent the Scouts from using public, tax-funded meeting places. Lynn Woolsey, a California Democrat who represents a portion of San Francisco, introduced legislation to revoke the Scouts federal charter, though the legislation was defeated.[12]

But why the repeated harassment of the Boy Scouts? Was it for some high and noble motive? Was it for the benefit of the boys in the Boy Scouts? Sears and Osten explain:

> The activists know the earlier they can influence young people the more effective they are in advancing their agenda. . . . Therefore, it is not too difficult to link homosexual behavior and predatory behaviors toward accessible teenage boys by those in positions of authority. The Scouts have genuine concern for those who are entrusted with the young men in their charge. As David Kupelian wrote, "The Scouting folks know what everyone with half a brain understands: that adults interested in sexual contact with young people gravitate toward careers and volunteer positions allowing proximity to their prey, positions such as coaches, teachers, scoutmasters—and priests."[13]

Is It Right to Silence a Message of Hope?

There are many sins and temptations all around us. We all live in a fallen world and a fallen world provides a host of evils that will entrap us if we are not careful. Homosexual sin is no better, or worse, than a host of other evils that destroy lives. Just as we do not believe that individuals are chosen to remain drug addicts, so too we do not believe that homosexuals are predetermined to remain homosexual. The view that some people are forever doomed to live destructive lifestyles has been contradicted over and over again. Dailey writes:

> Victory is possible. For every young man born into an impoverished, broken home and who becomes involved in illegal drugs, there are others who resist such temptations, choosing the right path. For every person who dies an early death from alcoholism, others gain the victory over the bottle. For every husband who surrenders to the "irresistible" enticement of sexual lust, many others learn to control such temptations and live faithful, monogamous lives.[14]

The tragedy of these religious harassment claims is that they are criminalizing those who offer homosexuals a way of escape from their tragic lifestyle. It's like making drug education illegal.

Under pressure from various advocacy groups laws are being made to silence Christians. Those who offer homosexuals lasting hope—that homosexuality is a sin but no one is locked into that lifestyle because Jesus can forgive sins and change our hearts—are being viewed as worthy of rebuke.

Should Christians Take Action?

While many Christians want to avoid conflict and offense, homosexual activists have no such qualms.

On April 25, 1993, some 300,000 gays and lesbians staged a march on Washington, D.C. It was a day when the homosexual community sought to flex its muscles. It was also a time of empowerment. Organizers scheduled hundreds of workshops and seminars to equip gays with everything they need to know. There were anti-racism workshops, a

"Lesbutante Ball," a congressional briefing on homosexuality in the black community, an ACT-UP civil disobedience action seminar, a choral festival put on by a national transgender caucus, a leather fetish conference, and many others, all events allegedly representing the full diversity of the gay, lesbian, and bisexual community.

There was also a complete disregard for decency and public decorum. According to one Park Service employee, the behavior of the crowd was shocking even by Washington standards:

> I thought I had seen it all. But I was entirely unprepared for this. Public nudity is one thing, but open, brazen sex acts, along the Washington mall, on the sidewalks, in the parks. . . . Well, I've just never seen anything like it. And I hope I never do again. I used to think that we should all be open-minded and just let people do what ever they want to do. But if this is what they have in mind: to turn our cities into a pornographic spectacle, well, they can just forget it.[15]

The media gave the event top billing. ABC News said the march was "one of the biggest civil rights demonstrations ever staged in the nation's capital." On the *MacNeil-Lehrer Report* the announcer said that the crowds gathered "to demand freedom from discrimination." NBC also gave the standard "party line" by reporting: "Organizers had a long list of demands. The top three: civil rights protection, an end to the ban on gays in the military, and more funding for AIDS research." But there were several things the media cleverly failed to report:

- Hundreds of lesbians who marched topless down Pennsylvania Avenue;
- Police orders not to arrest participants who violated public decency statutes;
- Topless women and nude men who cavorted, kissed, and embraced in the Navy Memorial Fountain;
- Lesbian marchers who filed past the White House chanting, "Chelsea, Chelsea, Chelsea!"

• Platform speakers who simulated sex acts on stage and roared out obscenities via giant amplifiers.[16]

How are Christians to respond to this blatant disregard for basic moral values? Are we to claim that these are political issues and that we are just supposed to pray and preach the Gospel?

Such an evasion of moral responsibility will not do. Jesus, Paul, along with the apostles and Hebrew prophets, addressed social and moral issues. They did not think in convenient categories of "political" and "religious" the way Christians often do today.

The idea of not addressing the evil behavior of a king or national ruler because that was in the realm of "politics" never occurred to Amos. God's men of old confronted evil in whatever form and wherever it was found. Some, as in the case of John the Baptist, paid with their lives. Even in our day, God's servants have suffered at the hands of ruthless political leaders, as was true of Titus Brandsma, a martyr who died at Dachau in 1942. His words still ring true: "Those who want to win the world for Christ must have the courage to come in conflict with it."[17]

Christians must educate themselves on the homosexual agenda and its conspiracy to take over society. Christians need to know what the Bible teaches on the subject, how to refute what the homosexual revisionists are saying about key biblical passages, and they need to vote for men and women of principle. Those who vote their "pocketbook" are totally selfish and obviously do not have "the mind of Christ."

Texas pastor Jack Graham addressed the Southern Baptist Convention, June 17, 2003, and elaborated on the words of Sir Winston Churchill. "To each," said Graham, "there comes in their lifetime a special moment when they are figuratively tapped on the shoulder and offered the chance to do a very special thing, unique to them and fitted to their talents. What a tragedy if that moment finds them unprepared and unqualified for that which could have been their finest hour."[18]

Christians are called to be salt and light (Matt. 5:13). It is the property of salt to penetrate, irritate, and stimulate. We must resist rottenness in order to combat decay. "It's not the bland leading the bland," said

Pastor Graham, but "flavorful, fresh believers full of the Spirit of God, pouring out the salty, tasty fresh love and grace of God."[19]

All too many Christians shy away from controversy and hope that the problem will, somehow, go away. They think that if they are just a little more patient everything will turn out all right. For those of my readers who think that way, and hope that the homosexual lobby will somehow forget its stated goals, the words of Winston Churchill are timely and to the point:

> If you will not fight for the right when you can easily win without blood-shed, if you will not fight when your victory will be sure and not too costly, you may come to the moment when you will have to fight with all odds against you and only a perilous chance for survival. Indeed, there may be a worse case. You may have to fight when there is no hope for victory, for it would be better to perish than to live as slaves.[20]

While many Christians do not approve of the homosexual lifestyle, they simply do not want to get "involved." Their refusal to oppose a homosexual takeover of our society by using legitimate means such as the ballot and the written word will lead to increasingly difficult days.

Trotsky once noted, "You may not be interested in war, but war is interested in you." In the same way, while many Christians are not interested in the Lavender Revolution, the Revolution is interested in them. And their children.

CHAPTER 5

Denying
the Health Problems

I will put none of these diseases upon thee.

—Exodus 15:26

In the Old Testament Scriptures, particularly in the Pentateuch, there are a variety of health and hygiene laws that were graciously given by God to His people because of His great love for them. These laws touched on practically every area of life from child birth to old age and death.

Moses, who was the spokesman for God and through whom God spoke to His people, had spent many years in Egypt. Though Moses was educated in the ways of the Egyptians (Acts 7:22) none of the Old Testament Mosaic legislation reflects the sometimes dangerous and harmful medical practices of the ancient Egyptians. Old Testament legislation clearly had its origin in God. It was in this way that God would protect His people from the diseases that were common in the pagan lands around them.

There is no question that God has, and can still heal miraculously.

Yet the promise of divine intervention in our health concerns was not given to lead us to ignore, and even violate, the principles of healthy living. The promise of Exodus 15:26 is given to those who pay attention to God's commandments and keep His laws, as the opening words of this verse indicate.

This is undoubtedly one of the reasons why God prohibited His people from committing homosexual acts (e.g. Lev. 18:22; 20:13). Though all prohibited sexual behaviors pose health problems, homosexual encounters, often involving multiple partners, are especially dangerous in this regard.

Extremely Risky Behavior

In a web article entitled "Why Reveal the Dark Side of the Gay Movement," Joseph Nicolosi tells why: "Statistics tell us that gay sex is often tied to substance abuse, promiscuity and unsafe sex practices. A significant minority of gay men also participate in sadomasochism, public sex in bathhouses and group sex."[1]

All of this means that homosexual behavior is unsafe and should not be promoted as a positive lifestyle. Dr. Gisela L. P. Macphail, a physician at the University of Calgary in Canada, addressed a letter to the Calgary Board of Education in 1996 and warned the school district of the dangers of promoting homosexuality in its classes. "Any practice which facilitates direct or indirect oral-rectal contact will enable the spread of fecal and rectal microorganisms to the sexual partner," wrote Dr. Macphail. "Thus anilingus . . . a common practice among homosexual men, allows direct spread of pathogens such as Giardia, Entamoeba histolytica, and Hepatitis A and of the typical STD organisms such as herpes simplex and gonorrhea."[2]

Both cancer and HIV are associated with homosexual practices. Dr. Stephen E. Goldstone, the medical director of GayHealth.com says he has found that 68 percent of HIV-positive and 45 percent of HIV-negative homosexual males have abnormal or precancerous anal cells.[3]

Homosexual encounters spread HIV. In 1998 the following report was filed:

In the U.S., anal intercourse continues to be the primary transmission route of HIV infection for homosexuals. The CDC says there are 40,000 new infections each year and the rate of infection is climbing because many younger homosexuals are engaging in risky behaviors. Many have become complacent about the epidemic because of new drugs that control the progression of the disease. As a result, homosexuals are staying alive longer and infecting more individuals. As of 1998, 54% of all HIV infections were homosexuals. An estimated 1 million Americans have been infected with HIV since it was first discovered in the 1980s. Worldwide, 21 million people have died; 450,000 Americans have died so far from HIV-related diseases.[4]

The "Thrill" of Public Places

Gay bathhouses—or, as they are ironically called, "health clubs"—are meeting places for gays who seem totally oblivious to the dangers from disease that they face with unknown partners. Lust overcomes reason and the inflamed individual plunges headlong over the precipice into a shortened lifespan filled with anguish.

Characteristically, homosexuality is noted for its rampant promiscuity between strangers: Men offering themselves to men and women offering themselves to women in public and private in the most perverse ways. Grant and Horne state: "Heterosexual activity, even at its most promiscuous, hardly comes close to homosexuality." And it is promiscuity that is marked by unbelievable frequency and fervor. "The sheer number of sexual encounters might militate against any passivity of tenderness, romance, and sensuality . . . the impersonal and mechanical anonymity utterly negates it."[5]

Private encounters with strangers is not exciting enough, however. Homosexuals are notorious for "taking over" parks, much to the chagrin of local residents. Public toilets are frequented especially by homosexual men, evidently because there is something appealing about sex in a public place where they might be discovered. Many men are even reluctant to use the public restrooms in areas of high homosexual activity. One observer writes:

Complaints have come from men who find that using the toilets means being either solicited or being witness to homosexual activity. Homosexual men have been attracted to the toilets at the University of Florida from as far as forty miles away. This university, as well as Dartmouth, Georgetown, and the University of California at San Diego, have been forced to install stainless steel panels between toilet stalls to prevent the drilling of holes in the walls for homosexual activity.[6]

AIDS— "The Unnecessary Epidemic"

Supposing you had a relative or friend who had a health problem producing some of the following symptoms:

- A decreased chance of enjoying a successful marriage;
- A five- to ten-year decrease in life expectancy from the general population;
- A chronic and potentially fatal liver disease, hepatitis;
- Pneumonia;
- Internal bleeding;
- Serious mental disabilities, many of which are irreversible;
- A much higher incidence of suicide from the general population;
- Inability to hold down a job;
- An only 30 percent likelihood of cure that can only come about through expensive, lengthy, and time-consuming treatment.

If you really cared for this person, and whether or not society considered this health problem to really be a problem, you would want this friend or relative to seek help. And even though there is no guarantee that treatment would be effective, you would suggest that this person give it a try.

What is this health problem described above? Alcoholism. It has been defined as a compulsive or addictive behavior that is hard to shake. The cure rate varies, depending on the motivation of the individual and several other factors such as social and genetic. Alcoholism has sparked many lively debates on the influence of nature and nurture, and which has a bigger role in alcoholism.

Now supposing you have another friend who has a condition with a similar list of emotional and physical problems:

- A significantly decreased chance of having a successful marriage;
- A 25- to 30-year reduction in life expectancy;
- A chronic, potentially fatal, liver disease—infectious hepatitis;
- A high risk of contracting a fatal disease that destroys the immune system (AIDS);
- Frequently fatal rectal cancer;
- A much higher incidence of suicide when compared to the general population;
- No guarantee of successful treatment, although a very high success rate, in some cases nearing 100 percent for highly motivated, carefully selected individuals.

In these two hypothetical conditions, the first alcoholism and the second homosexuality, we find many parallels. Dr. Jeffrey Satinover, M.D., points out that "despite the parallels between the two conditions, what is striking today are the sharply different responses to them."[7]

According to the figures cited earlier in this chapter, AIDS, a fatal disease associated with the homosexual lifestyle, has reached epidemic proportions. It is interesting to observe how societies have dealt with epidemics.

During the plague epidemic of fourteenth-century Europe some 25 million people died. The populations of cities and towns were literally decimated as one individual after another became ill and then succumbed to the "Black Death." History records that in an attempt to deal with the problem whole sections of cities were burned to the ground and villages razed. Sickened individuals were isolated until they improved or passed on.

In the fifteenth and sixteenth centuries there were outbreaks of syphilis. In an attempt to contain the outbreaks, governments shut down brothels and houses of ill-repute. The health of the population was considered as a primary concern and whatever action was necessary to preserve it was taken without apology.

The influenza epidemic that followed WW I took the lives of some 20 million people. Individuals wore face masks, public gathering places were closed, and important meetings were cancelled. Here, too, rigorous but necessary steps were taken to preserve the general health of the population.

In the 1930s syphilis again reared its ugly head. The United States Surgeon General made an intensive effort to curtail its spread and encouraged doctors to do routine Wasserman testing on all patients who came to them for whatever reason. The circle of testing was expanded through a program of premarital and prenatal testing. Infected patients were identified and effort was made to trace and to contact any sexual partners who may have been exposed to the disease.[8]

Recently, though "only" some 3,000 people died from SARS worldwide—a miniscule number compared to AIDS deaths—yet drastic precautions were taken. The nightly news showed office workers in Far Eastern cities, commuters and travelers, all wearing facial masks. Schools and public places were closed down. Suspected victims were isolated until test results could be verified.

But why aren't similar preventative measures being taken with regard to HIV? Why is the homosexual lifestyle—the major propagator of AIDS—being encouraged by the U.S. Supreme Court? Why is the media glorifying this lifestyle and desensitizing the population of the world to the horrible health risks associated with homosexual encounters?

In his book *AIDS: The Unnecessary Epidemic*, Dr. Stanley Monteith, M.D., traces the AIDS epidemic from its inception and notes the number of unusual developments in *this* epidemic that show it to be not just an epidemic, but a politicized one.

On June 5, 1981, the first published report in American medical literature describing a deadly new disease affecting homosexual men was published by the Centers for Disease Control and called "the Plague of the Twentieth Century." On July 3, 1981, the CDC announced twenty-six cases of Kaposi's Sarcoma (KS) in homosexual men along with ten additional cases of Pneumocystis pneumonia (PCP). Some of the gay patients were developing both KS and PCP. What was significant was that the common denominator between KS and PCP cases was a suppressed immunological system (AIDS). According to Monteith:

> Soon thereafter, a myriad of rare diseases began infecting homosexuals. There were infections with the cytomegalo virus producing blindness, infection with the herpes virus producing horribly painful shingles, infections with yeasts and fungus, infections of the brain, bowel, heart and of almost every other organ system. There were strange and exotic diseases that had rarely attacked humans before. Tuberculosis began to appear with increasing frequency in the helpless young men. Peripheral neuritis and dementia destroyed their nervous systems.[9]

In October of 1981 the CDC realized that there was an emerging problem of gigantic proportions that threatened the health of every American. Using careful interview procedures CDC epidemiologists interviewed AIDS patients and sought to trace their sexual partners for the five years prior to the appearance of symptoms. For those who had already died, companions and friends of the deceased were contacted and interviewed. What appeared to be a common denominator was that the patients who had AIDS: (1) met their partners in gay bathhouses; (2) engaged in sex acts unique to homosexuals.[10]

In addition to these two commonalities for most of the AIDS patients, interviewers also found that one man could be directly, or indirectly, traced to at least 40 cases of AIDS from New York City to various locations in Southern California. The man, Gaetan Dugas, a French Canadian airline steward, claimed that he had approximately 250 different sexual partners every year from 1979 to 1981.

Gaetan Dugas seemed to have a callous indifference to the woe he was bringing to the men he had contact with. Homosexual journalist Randy Shilts writes of Gaetan Dugas, the individual whom many consider to be "patient zero," the individual who first brought AIDS to America.

> Gaetan Dugas' eyes flashed but without their usual charm, when Selma Dritz [a public health worker] bluntly told him he must stop going to the bathhouses. The hotline at the Kaposi's Sarcoma foundation was receiving repeated calls from people complaining of a man with a French accent who was having sex with people at various sex parlors and then calmly telling them he had gay cancer. It was one of the most repulsive things Dritz had heard in her nearly forty years in public health: "It's none of your _____ business!" said Gaetan. "It's my right to do what I want with my own body."
>
> "It's not your right to go out and give other people disease," Dritz replied, keeping her professional calm. "Then you make decisions for their bodies, not yours."
>
> "It's their duty to protect themselves," said the airline steward. "They know what's going on here. They've heard about this disease."
>
> Dritz tried to reason further but got nowhere.
>
> "I've got it," Gaetan said angrily. "They can get it too."[11]

The statistics show that HIV-AIDS infections are skyrocketing among homosexuals, yet there is little warning, if any, given to homosexuals. Gay advocacy groups have access to the same statistics as I have cited. They know the risks and dangers, yet advocacy groups push their deadly lifestyle and try to promote it among the young and the unsuspecting.

While homosexuals are not warned about the health risks they face they are reminded in gay publications and by gay leaders that there is a real danger of quarantine for anyone infected with or suspected of being infected with the virus.

The dark specter of quarantine is used to reinforce homosexual fears that they will soon be rounded up and incarcerated. These fears were reinforced by Lyndon LaRouche's ballot initiatives in California in 1986 and 1988 and his talking about the necessity of quarantine. This has led many homosexuals to believe that anyone who wanted reporting and public health monitoring of the disease favored quarantine. But according to Monteith, "All responsible medical authorities have agreed that quarantine is not necessary to stop this epidemic—except for those people who are intentionally spreading the disease."[12]

In his *AIDS: The Unnecessary Epidemic*, Monteith observes that liberal politicians claim that AIDS education is the best way to deal with the epidemic, yet this education process is seriously flawed.

Education on homosexuality never tells our children what homosexuals really do. It only serves to convince them how nice and pleasant homosexuals are. The fact that 25% of homosexuals practice sadomasochism or that the North American Man-Boy Love Association (NAMBLA) consisting of homosexual pedophiles is actively seducing your children is never mentioned.

Children are never told that homosexual practices lead directly to Hepatitis B infection, a massive incidence of venereal disease and a compulsive, addictive lifestyle with severe emotional problems. Children are never told of the high suicide rates among homosexuals or the sadness and isolation felt by these tragic people. They are educating our children only about the positive aspects of the homosexual lifestyle in order to encourage the curiosity of youth and lead our young people into the homosexual way of death.[13]

Second Hand Smoke and First Hand AIDS

As of late politicians have been winning favor with their constituents by showing their outrage at the tobacco industry. Citing the tragedy of a close friend who died a horrible death from lung cancer or some other smoking-related health problem, Republicans and Democrats alike wax eloquent in their tirades against the health risks and consequent burden on the health-care system caused by tobacco. Others are claiming that secondhand smoke is only superseded in lethality by mozzarella on pizza, which is bad for your circulatory system.

In a *WorldNetDaily* commentary Mychal S. Massie makes some significant points about class-action lawsuits against the fast-food and to-bacco industries. Entitled "If health costs are key, why not sue sodomists?" Massie raises some valid points.

Ronald McDonald House Charities was named one of America's best charities of 2002. The organization awarded more than $340 million in grants to various children's programs. McDonald's Restaurants employs over 1.5 million people worldwide. "But," says Massie, "how many jobs have sodomist organizations created?"

Massie also observes that the cigarette industry pours millions into racing, the marketing of the races, and the facilities, all of which means jobs and money for the local community. Yet, suit after suit is leveled at the tobacco industry, and this despite the warning clearly written on cigarette packaging. How about some lawsuits against gay organizations for promoting another really dangerous lifestyle? "Irresponsible dangerous sexual practices and intravenous drug abuse are a greater financial burden to every facet of the health-care system than is a double bacon cheeseburger with a Marlboro chaser," observes Massie.[14]

I certainly do not want to promote smoking, unhealthy eating practices, or anything else which is not glorifying to God, but Massie has a point. Why are we picking only on certain organizations that create health problems while ignoring others?

What Will It Take?

Following the terrible tragedy of 9-11, many Americans began to think about America's future. On an almost daily basis new threats were being announced, and then came the deaths from anthrax. Added to this has been the news that the North Koreans are developing nuclear weapons and also systems for their delivery.

Will America be brought down by an armed invasion from without, or by Islamic fanatics on our shores? Or is our possible national demise from some other, even more sinister source?

In June of 1838, Abraham Lincoln gave an address to the Lyceum in Springfield, Illinois. One portion of the address is terribly relevant to the subject of this book.

At what point should we expect the approach of danger? By what means should we fortify ourselves against it? Should we expect some transatlantic military giant to step the ocean and crush us with a blow? Never! All the armies of Europe and Asia and Africa combined, could never, by force, take a drink from the Ohio or make a mark on the Blue Ridge, not in a thousand years.

Then at what point should danger be expected? I answer: If it ever reach us, it must spring up among us. It can never come from abroad. If destruction be our lot, then we ourselves must be its author and its finisher. As a nation of free men, we must live on through all time, or die by suicide.[15]

PART II

The Rage

CHAPTER 6

Redesigning Society

And he shall speak great words against the most High . . . and think to
change times and laws.

—Daniel 7:25

Daniel 7 reveals four beasts who represent four future kings coming
upon the earth (vs. 17). The text focuses on the fourth beast and
tells us that he "shall devour the whole earth, and shall tread it down,
and break it in pieces" (vs. 23).

Here is a picture of savagery and destruction. This beast devours, he
treads down, and he breaks. Can we even begin to grasp the meaning of
this prophetic text?

There is a particular detail that is given. It's the mouth of this fourth
beast: "And he shall speak great words against the most High." He is a
blasphemer. And not only does he speak *against* God, but he seeks to
subvert and then redesign the divine order: He will seek "to change times
and laws."

In the Spirit of Antichrist

In a recent article in *The New American* entitled "Unmentionable Vice Goes

Mainstream," William Norman Grigg argues that "homosexuality's rapid rise from unmentionable vice to celebrated minority status is part of a campaign to subvert Judeo-Christian culture."[1]

Grigg is right on target. The homosexual agenda is not a mere cultural phenomenon—one out of many— but a well-organized and well-financed strategy to change culture and transform society.

Paul Ettelbrick, former legal director of the Lambda Legal Defense and Education Fund, has stated: "Being queer is more than setting up house, sleeping with a person of the same gender, and seeking state approval for doing so. . . . Being queer means pushing the parameters of sex, sexuality, and family, and in the process transforming the very fabric of society."[2]

The homosexual agenda is the advance guard in the culture war. It is driven by a desire to strike out against all of the traditional values that the homosexual perceives have brought suffering to him or her. The agenda's militant approach in bringing an unhealthy lifestyle to society shows that homosexuality is both a tragedy and a threat.

Redesigning Society Through Education

Not only are gays infiltrating secondary schools and working on the minds of children, but they have gotten a number of pro-gay courses on to college campuses and into college curriculums. The following is but a small sample.

+ Black Lavender: A Study of Black Gay and Lesbian Plays, and Dramatic Constructions in American Theatre (Brown University)
+ Discourses of Desire: Introduction to Gay and Lesbian Studies (Columbia University)
+ Science, Technology and Queer Theory (Yale University)
+ Lesbian Communities and Identities (Stanford University)
+ Lesbian Novels Since World War II (Swarthmore University)
+ Queer Media (Swarthmore University)

- Representations of Lesbians and Gay Men in Popular Culture (Georgetown University)
- Lesbian/Bisexual Women's Theories/Lives/Activisms (University of Arizona)
- Lesbian Lives in the U.S. (University of Iowa)
- Feminist Perspectives on Lesbian Studies: Crossing Erotic Boundaries (University of Michigan)
- Gay Men and Homophobia in American Culture (University of Minnesota)
- Lesbian/Queer Cultural Production (University of Minnesota)
- Backgrounds of Homoerotic Literature (Rutgers University)
- Issues in Lesbian and Gay Visual Representation (University of California—Irvine)
- Queer Textuality (University of California—Santa Barbara)[3]

Some state universities are actually promoting homosexuality in their English classes. Ben Shapiro reports on a course taught at the University of Michigan, Ann Arbor. The title of the course: "How To Be Gay: Male Homosexuality and Initiation." The course, English 317, is described as follows: "This course will examine the general topic of the role that initiation plays in the formation of gay male identity. . . . In particular, we will examine a number of cultural artifacts and activities that seem to play a prominent role in learning how to be gay: [including] camp, diva-worship, drag, muscle, culture, taste, style and political activism."

Other state universities, such as the University of Pennsylvania and the University of Maryland, also introduce students to gay and lesbian literature in college English courses. English 265, taught at the University of Maryland, is described as "a study of the pervasiveness of homo-eroticism in literature from the Renaissance to the present."[4]

Falsehood Presented as Truth

Gay studies are presented in an academic context that reinforces their content and their world-and-life view. The Christian world-and-life view is ridiculed and subject to attack. Students often hear professors say:

"While you are taking this course you are to leave your religious beliefs home. This is not a Sunday school class, and you can't run to your parents, or your preacher, for answers to hard questions." Other students are told by the prof, "I don't mind students having sincere religious beliefs but check your religious hats at the door. We are interested in empirical evidence in this class, not personal beliefs."

Of course, the good professor is ignorant of the fact that such statements are actually statements of his/her own personal religious beliefs. There is no religious neutrality. Even atheists have their own final standard: themselves. Nevertheless, many students are intimidated by the professor with his impressive list of credentials and degrees after his or her name at the back of the college catalog. The whole setting is intimidating and is calculated to allow the religious beliefs of the professors to be cleverly transferred to the minds of the students who think they are getting science and the objective truth when, in fact, they are getting another religious view. It is in such an intellectually dishonest environment that unsuspecting students are often led to buy into the homosexual agenda or to at least be tolerant of great evil.

A gay or lesbian professor can have an unfair advantage over immature young men and women in an educational setting where there are no moral restraints. In such a setting, cut off from rational restrictions, emotion, opinion, and false impression rule. Students are young and susceptible. Students who claim that are gay can easily be persuaded that gays are treated unfairly. The result is that many students experience anger and self-pity. In some cases both teachers and students form an indissoluble bond and commiserate together about "our homophobic society."

Reinforcing Evil Through Isolation
Who takes these college courses in gay and lesbian studies? Students who are sympathetic to gay and lesbian perspectives. Such students study the gay and lesbian culture often in highly flattering and historically inaccurate settings. Students who are immersed in such a culture, and who live in an on-campus dormitory setting that is pro-gay, socialize

only with members of that particular group. Such students do not acquire the knowledge and social skills necessary to deal comfortably with heterosexuals. As is true with many so-called multi-cultural groups, multi-culturalism becomes an excuse for greater and greater isolation.

Gender Neutral Dorms

Many American colleges and universities have bought into the gay agenda and are supportive of its goals. Some are currently appealing to gay, bisexual, and transgender students by having admissions forms with check-off boxes so that students can indicate their sexual orientation. More and more are featuring coed dormitories with men and women living on the same floor. Some have taken this a step further and have coed dorm rooms. At two high-name colleges, homosexual groups claimed that it was "heterosexist" to require roommates to be of the same sex. In order to avoid undue tension and confusion—or so goes the argument—gay men should be allowed to room with females.[5]

Then there are the bathrooms. Some schools are seeking to provide "gender neutral" bathrooms in order to "protect" certain students from possible harassment. Other schools proudly boast that they are concerned with the rights of gay, bisexual, and transgender students. But what about the rights of the heterosexual student? Don't normal people have any rights? Sears and Osten state:

> The right of the homosexual to have housing that makes him or her feel comfortable trumps the right of a heterosexual young man and young woman to have housing that does not place them in either a sexually tempting or sexually compromising environment. In addition, those individuals who have religious objections to homosexual behavior and therefore would rather not live with someone who practices homosexual behavior are labeled "homophobes" or have their requests fall on deaf ears.[6]

There are cases where the rights of Christians and other religious conservatives are infringed in favor of the rights of others, or at least brought into question and challenged. In *Rader v. The University of Nebraska*, a Christian student wanted to move out of student housing because of the offensive (from the Christian student's point of view) behaviors of other dorm students. The problem, however, is that the University of Nebraska requires that students live in the dorms. In another case, two Orthodox Jewish students wanted to leave the dorms because their Jewish beliefs clashed with the behaviors of other students.

The Christian student enjoyed a victory as the court affirmed the validity of the student's beliefs while the two Jewish students lost their case. Unfortunately, such conflicts are becoming more frequent in our homoeroticized society. Sad to say "while people of faith find themselves forced to put up with behavior that offends them, those who practice homosexual behavior are catered to, at the expense of everyone else."[7]

Redesigning Society Through the Media

Media Bias

The advance of the homosexual cause can be attributed in large measure to the media. The media has been responsible for playing up gay rights and deliberately distorting information about conservative Christians and others who hold to a position of opposition against the homosexual agenda. A prime example is how the media drummed up interest in allocating money for AIDS research. This is one of the most amazing stories as told by CBS insider Bernard Goldberg.

Media movers and shakers knew that they had to do something to get the average American man or woman interested in AIDS research and willing to contact their representatives to request more money be allocated to AIDS research. The problem, however, is that AIDS research is not really a high priority item with your average American man or woman. AIDS is associated with homosexual practices and since most Americans are not homosexual, there was very little perceived need to spend money on this cause.

What could be done? How could your average American see that this is a real problem, *their* problem? Start announcing that the same disease that was doing in junkies and gay men was now spreading to chaste housewives and baseball dads all around the country. The guy that coaches Little League could come down with AIDS just like the gay man frequenting bathhouses.

The plan was to lead people to believe that AIDS was striking everyone. Scare everyone to death and claim that YOU could come down with AIDS. Then, maybe, people would be interested. "Otherwise," writes CBS insider Bernard Goldberg in his book *Bias*, "the activists feared, there would never be a national outcry over AIDS. Middle America would never get worked up enough—and neither would Congress and the president—to spend whatever it took to combat this modern-day plague. As long as the people dying were mostly gay men and junkies, the AIDS lobby had a problem."[8]

Who would help the AIDS lobby in selling America the untrue idea that AIDS was a common disease? The "compassionate" media. While AIDS was taking a severe toll among gays and junkies, the battle cry became "No One Is Safe Anymore—Even You!" Once the media was able to create its own reality, the door was open to convincing heterosexuals and faithful moms that they too could be afflicted with AIDS.

Goldberg lists several headlines and front covers to show how this played out.

- *U.S. News & World Report* claimed: "The disease of THEM is suddenly the disease of US."
- *USA Today* ran this alarming headline: "Cases Rising Fastest Among Heterosexuals."
- *Time* reported: "The proportion of heterosexual cases . . . is increasing at a worrisome rate. . . . The numbers as yet are small, but AIDS is a growing threat to the heterosexual population."
- *Atlantic Monthly* featured this cover story: "Heterosexuals and AIDS: The Second State of the Epidemic."
- *Ladies Home Journal* ran a tease headline: "AIDS & Marriage: What Every Wife Must Know."
- In 1987 Oprah Winfrey, mogul and sage for so many Americans, stated: "AIDS has both sexes running scared. Research

studies now project that one in five—listen to me, hard to believe—one in five heterosexuals could be dead from AIDS at the end of the next three years. That's by 1990. One in five. It is no longer just a gay disease. Believe me."[9]

"Jesse Who? . . ."

While most Americans have heard of Matthew Shepard, the young Wyoming homosexual who was murdered by two men who were supposedly "fundamentalist Christian," most have not heard the name of Jesse Dirkhising, who was murdered by two homosexuals, Joshua Brown and Dennis Carpenter. The Shepard story will endure on into the future as a symbol of bigotry and intolerance. The latter, however, has been virtually ignored. A webpage devoted to these two murders gives the following survey of events.

Brent Bozell, "No Media Memorial for Jesse Dirkhising"—

In this modern media age, when lurid murders, especially of children, dance in the dreams of ratings-obsessed network producers (can you say Jon Benet?), why would this story go untold? Had Jesse Dirkhising been shot inside his Arkansas school, he would have been an immediate national news story. Had he been openly gay and his attackers heterosexual, the crime would have led all the networks. But no liberal media outlet would dare be the first to tell a grisly murder story which has as its villains two gay men.

The Federalist, October 29, 1999—

. . . the print and boob-tube disinformers are ablaze with "hate" headlines. The trial of those in the racially motivated murder of a black man in Texas by several white men, and the trial of those who murdered a homosexual man in Wyoming, are all the rage. But consider the following stories, which have not made headlines for reasons that will become obvious:

In the Wyoming case, "The death of Matthew Shepard last year shocked the nation and led to calls for stronger laws against hate crimes," proclaims CNN. So, you have heard about Jesse Dirkhising, the 13-year-old boy who was raped, tortured, and murdered in Prairie Grove, Ark., last month by a 22-year-old homosexual and his 38-year-old "lover"?

Question of the week . . . "Joe, since the President spoke out so commendably about the murder of adult homosexual Matt Shepard in Wyoming, I'm wondering what was his reaction to the repeated rape and murder of 13-year-old Jesse Dirkhising by two adult homosexual men in Arkansas," asked Baltimore radio personality Les Kinsolving. White House spokesman Joe Lockhart responded, "I don't know that the President is aware of that circumstance." Mr. Kinsolving then asked, "As his media adviser, were you surprised that while the murder of an adult, Shepard, received enormous coverage in the big media, this multiple rape and murder of a child went so widely unreported?" Lockhart responded, "I try to keep my media criticisms to myself."[10]

Most Americans (shame on them!) get their news from the general media. Media moguls know this and are having a field day creating the reality that they want to project. While most Americans consider themselves well-informed, they are really not. "All the news that's fit to print" really means "all the news that the media elite slant is only fit to print."

Redesigning Society Through the Military

Military Law

Homosexual activists are working diligently to change the current, official ban on gays in the military.

The present law against homosexuals serving in the military was passed in 1993. This made the historical prohibition against military service for homosexuals a matter of statute law. William Clinton's "don't-ask-don't-tell" policy is not official military law. It "was the result of a compromise between the President, who had failed in his attempt to lift the ban on homosexuals serving openly in the military, and the Joint Chiefs of Staff and key members of Congress, who adamantly opposed lifting the ban. The policy does not have the force of law and could be repealed at the stroke of a pen."[11]

There have been several attempts to change military law. Some have asserted that a ban on gays in the military is unenforceable, and therefore useless. The continuing persistence of gays in the military, supposedly, is proof that this is an unenforceable matter. Yet, there has been a continuing persistence of malingerers, slovenliness, and disrespect for authority. If the persistence argument is valid, then there ought to be no military regulations against malingerers, slovenliness, and disrespect for authority.

Military law currently requires that homosexuals who are so identified by their acts, or by their own admission, must be separated from military service. But doesn't this violate an individual's constitutional rights and isn't such a law un-American?

While this question is frequently raised, this law does not infringe on anyone's constitutional rights because there is no constitutional right to serve in the military. According to the findings of Congress as expressed in the legislation:

- Success in combat depends on military units characterized by high morale, good order and discipline, and unit cohesion.
- Military life is fundamentally different from civilian life. Because of the unique conditions service members face and the unique responsibilities that military service entails, the military community constitutes a specialized society governed by its own laws, rules, customs, and traditions, including restrictions on personal behavior that would be unacceptable in civilian society. Standards of conduct apply to military members at all times, whether on or off duty, whether on base or off.
- Homosexuality is incompatible with military service and presents a risk to the morale, good order and discipline, and unit cohesion that underpins military effectiveness. Officers and NCOs who have the responsibility for maintaining military effectiveness should have great discretion concerning what constitutes sufficient information upon which to question a service member regarding his or her status as a homosexual.[12]

A Civil Rights Issue?

Despite the determination of Congress and military leaders, there are many who treat the issue of gays in the military as the latest phase in the struggle for civil rights. They often cite President Truman's executive order after WW II that racially integrated the U.S. military. A few years ago the *Boston Globe* stated that "today's soldiers and sailors reluctant to serve shoulder to shoulder with homosexuals are the progeny of racist and sexist soldiers and sailors who were told to get over it or get out."[13]

But is it true that this is a civil rights issue? Many believe so and equate opposition to permitting homosexuals to serve openly in the military with opposition to racial integration. However, the similarities cited are not valid ones. Former chairman of the Joint Chiefs of Staff, Gen. Colin Powell, drew the proper distinction in a reply to former Rep. Pat Schroeder (D-Colo), when she debated the point with him. Powell stated: "Skin color is a benign non-behavioral characteristic. Sexual orientation is perhaps the most profound of human behavioral characteristics. Comparison of the two is a convenient but invalid argument." Powell stated, in his testimony before Congress in 1992, that "it would be prejudicial to good order and discipline to try to integrate [open homosexuals] into the current military structure."[14]

The Lawrence Precedent

In a *CNSNews.com* report (October 9, 2003) entitled "Sodomy Ban Places Military Code at Odds with Supreme Court Precedent," Steve Brown relates how the *Lawrence* v. *Texas* decision actually places the United States Supreme Court at odds with official U.S. military law.

Article 125 of the Uniform Code of Military Justice (UCMJ)—known as "the sodomy statute" because it bans sodomy among members of the armed forces—is being targeted by the Servicemembers Legal Defense Network (SLDN) on the basis of the *Lawrence* decision. Referring to *U.S. v. Marcum*, which involves Air Force Technical Sergeant Eric Marcum, who was convicted of performing consensual sodomy with a male airman in his home, Steve Ralls, SLDN spokesman, stated: "If the court elects to follow the Supreme Court's *Lawrence* decision and strike down

Article 125, that would have a far-reaching effect within the military not only for lesbian and gay service members, but for heterosexual service members as well."

Ralls referenced a Rand Institute study which suggests that as many as 80 percent of *heterosexual* service members engage in private consensual sodomy. "So it's not limited to just gay and lesbian service members," stated Ralls, "but a very sizable portion of the military population."

Lessons from the Past

Allowing practicing homosexuals in the military will harm the morale and efficiency of the military—something that is critical in days when America is under the continuing threat of terrorist attack.

Though homosexual activists argue differently, legitimizing homosexuality in the military will have dire consequences for American security. Given the aggressive nature of homosexual promiscuity, allowing practicing gays in close quarters with other individuals of the same sex could provide tremendous unrest and fear. Should we be making the military safe for homosexuals, or should we be making the military safe for men and women who wish to serve their country as best they can? The following account shows how unsettling an aggressive homosexual assault can be.

In 1945 a young recruit was sound asleep during his first night aboard ship when he was abruptly disturbed. "The awakening was sudden and panic-filled. A hand was caressing my leg, running up the inside of my thigh. A dim figure ducked away as I lashed out, kicking, swinging a fist and striking the air. There was no more sleep that night."

Kevin McCrane, now a retired businessman living in New Jersey, had been drafted into the navy at the close of World War II. In January he was assigned with four others to the USS *Warrick*, a cargo carrier. The day after McCrane was sexually harassed, the ship set sail for Honolulu. "But the excitement was gone, at least for me. At the end of a long day riding the sea's rolling swells, I took a twelve-inch, box-end wrench from the engine room and retreated to my berth. Hanging onto the wrench under my pillow, I slept."[15]

Unfortunately, the moral corruption of a society must also adversely affect the men and women in the military. Even with special safeguards the military will never be able to enjoy a complete immunity from the vices of society. The homosexual takeover is not only a health problem. It also presents a security risk. Weakened by gays in the military, it will not be long before a nation of sodomites will crumble before a disciplined enemy. Lieutenant Commander Gerry Carroll has stated:

> I can imagine few things more destructive to the military—upon which we have depended for two hundred years for the safety and security of our way of life—than to integrate homosexuals into it. Forcing young service men and women to live in the close contact of others with a chosen lifestyle that is utterly repugnant to them will ultimately put this nation in the position of countries like France and the Netherlands, who speak loudly but carry not stick at all.[16]

The "Coming Out" of a Conspiracy

There can be little doubt that homosexual activists are seeking to restructure society and to impose their values on everyone else. There is a national and international conspiracy in operation that is quietly working behind the scenes. Lately, the conspiracy has itself had a "coming out." Emboldened by recent successes in government and law gay activists no longer feel that they need to keep their purposes secret. They are even filling the ranks of the Republican Party, generally perceived to be conservative.

Two pro-gay groups, the Log Cabin Republicans and the Republican Unity Coalition, are playing a more dominant role in the party. In a report by John Cloud entitled "The New Face of Gay Power" and appearing in *Time* for October 13, 2003, we read: "If you want to understand the future of gay politics, forget Fire Island, N.Y., and West Hollywood, Calif. Come instead to Cody, Wyo., at Yellowstone's doorstep, where a national gay-straight alliance, the Republican Unity Coalition (RUC), was founded two years ago and counts former President Gerald Ford among its board members."

A scenic drive down the road from Cody, you come to Casper, Wyoming, the hometown of Vice President Dick Cheney who has graciously and publicly accepted his openly lesbian daughter Mary. It's also where Guy Padgett III, a member of the city council, decided to "come out" recently and declare his gay orientation. You can also take another scenic drive through the Medicine Bow National Forest to Laramie, now known as "the Berkley of Wyoming." It is the only "city" in the state that can boast a four-year university and is home to Spectrum, labeled by John Cloud in the *Time* article "one of the most vibrant gay college groups in the West." When Russell Henderson and Aaron McKinney murdered Matthew Shepard, they murdered more than a young homosexual.

The RUC was founded by the Bush family friend, Charles Francis. "Francis wanted to start an organization that would institutionalize the ties between well-connected gay Republicans like himself and the straight party leadership. It would be a 'grass-tops' group that would complement a grass-roots organization called the Log Cabin Republicans." Francis picked Cody's Alan Simpson, a prominent straight Republican who left the U.S. Senate in 1997 after an eighteen-year career, to be chairman.

The "credo" of the RUC is the Cody Statement, so titled because it was signed in the basement of Cody's Buffalo Bill Historical Center in August of 2001. In part the Cody Statement declares, as recorded in the *Time* article:

> We are Republican because we believe in limited government, free markets, a strong national defense, and personal responsibility. . . . Some of us are straight, some of us are gay or lesbian, and some of us think it is nobody's business but our own what we are. All of us are American.

Could "the land of the free and the home of the brave" become "the land of the gay and the home of the transgendered"?

CHAPTER 7

Reinterpreting the Bible

Yea, hath God said? . . .   —Genesis 3:1

C hristians everywhere regard the Bible as our ultimate and final authority. What it says, God says. To disobey the Bible is to disobey
God. Because the Bible is so important in determining what is right and
wrong, it is not at all surprising that homosexual revisionists have gone
out of their way to show that the Bible does not condemn all homosexuality. Revisionists claim that conservatives and traditionalists only think
that it does, but they think that way because they haven't read the Bible
correctly.

This is probably the most effective tool of homosexual revisionists.
Most of the opposition to the gay agenda in America comes from the
Christian right. Christians of all persuasions—Pentecostal to Reformed
and everything in between—cite Scripture to show what God thinks of
homosexuality. Revisionists also cite Scripture to show what God *really*
thinks of it. After all, if God approves of the lifestyle, what Christian
would dare to oppose it?

Oxford's Gay Bible

The *New Oxford Annotated Bible,* third edition, has radically reinterpreted key sections of Scripture. As a result, the third edition has negated basic Christian beliefs about homosexuality, the deity of Jesus Christ, and the sanctity of human life. The *New Oxford Annotated Bible*, third edition, is a racy, politically correct commentary using the text of the gender-inclusive New Revised Standard Version of the Bible.

Troy D. Perry, founder of the homosexual Metropolitan Community Churches (MCC) wrote a glowing commendation of the notes and annotations. He stated:

> I am excited to share with you today one of the most important theological breakthroughs in the 33-year history of Metropolitan Community Churches. . . . The world renowned biblical scholars who prepared *The New Oxford Annotated Bible* have adopted a great deal of MCCs own scholarship and theology: There is no biblical condemnation of homosexuality—only prohibitions against its misuse, just as there is no biblical blanket condemnation of heterosexuality, only prohibitions against misuse of that gift.[1]

It is at this point that gay revisionist theologians present perhaps their most important and critical challenge. Homosexual theology claims to be thoroughly biblical and is advanced by individuals who have had graduate and post-graduate training in biblical theology, the biblical languages, church history, and ancient history. Most Christians are ill-prepared to deal with their scholarly and well thought out arguments and end up saying something like "God created Adam and Eve, not Adam and Steve." Statements like this are of no avail. Erroneous homosexual exegesis must be countered by sound biblical exegesis.

The task is difficult. A former homosexual activist who had been working to advance gay theology explains the difficulty. He uses Matthew 11:28 where Jesus says: "Come unto me, all ye that labor and are heavy laden and I will give you rest." "Do you know what that means?" he asks. Well, most Christians would answer "yes." Then he asks a revealing question:

Now suppose someone tells you they have done an extensive word study on this verse, and discovered Jesus was *really* inviting pregnant women to stay at His maternity ward in Nazareth. It seems ridiculous; the context so clearly points to something else. But if you have not taken the time to study the original Greek in this verse, you cannot technically refute the "maternity ward" idea, though common sense tells you it is nonsense.

This is the power of the pro-gay theology. It takes scriptures we are all familiar with, gives them an entirely new interpretation, backs its claims with well-credentialed scholars, and gives birth to a new sexual ethic. Common sense may reject it, but until it is examined a bit more closely, it is difficult to refute.[2]

Revisionists and the Creation Account

Most Christians believe that the creation account shows that God created Adam and Eve and created them to have children and build families. From the start, traditionalists believe that they have Scripture on their side.

While they do, revisionists make a simple matter complicated and do not surrender so easily. They argue that at the beginning heterosexual union was necessary for there to be offspring and descendants of the first couple. However, they argue that reproduction is not the model for all couples since there are many couples in a traditional marriage arrangement who cannot have children. Are they sinning because they are childless? Moreover, revisionists would argue that the creation account never condemns homosexual relations.

Yet while it is true that the early chapters of Genesis do not prohibit homosexuality, neither do they prohibit wife-beating and infanticide. We should point out that while the creation account does not condemn homosexuality, it provides the only model for sexual activity which is consistently advocated throughout biblical history. The heterosexual model of Adam and Eve is reinforced over and over again; that which is contrary to the model (homosexuality, pederasty, bestiality) is repeatedly condemned. While heterosexual monogamous marriages are praised and are used as a reflection of the love of Christ for His church, homosexual relationships are never used as a model of anything good. Certain types of heterosexual arrangements are condemned—fornication and adultery—but *all* types of homosexual arrangements are uniformly treated as sin. The message of the Bible is: "Be faithful to the wife of your youth." The Bible never says "be faithful to the homosexual lover of your youth."

And what about heterosexual couples who are childless? There is a vast difference between homosexual couples who are childless because they are a same-sex couple and never intended to produce offspring, and a heterosexual couple who normally would have children but cannot. They *cannot*, but the homosexual couple *would not*. The impediment is in the intention of the same-sex couple.

Most Christians find it hard to believe that homosexuals would use the Bible to justify the homosexual lifestyle. Joe Dallas writes:

> I remember clearly, and with inexpressible regret, the day I convinced myself it was acceptable for me to be both gay and Christian. Not only did I embrace the pro-gay theology—I promoted it well, serving on the staff of the local Metropolitan Community Church and presenting the arguments cited in this series. Twelve years have passed since I realized my error, and during those years the pro-gay theology has enjoyed unprecedented exposure and acceptance, both in mainline denominations and among sincere (albeit sincerely deceived) believers.
>
> Many Christians are unaware that there is such a thing as pro-gay theology, much less a movement built around it. And many who are aware of it have no idea how to answer its claims. Yet an answer is required; the pro-gay theology, like the gay rights movement it represents, grows daily in scope and influence. With the love Christ showed while weeping over Jerusalem, and the anger He displayed when clearing the Temple, the Church must respond.[3]

Wresting Scripture: The Whys and Wherefores

Adolph Hitler, Jim Jones, cult leaders around the world, and even the devil himself love to quote Scripture. People have a mystical reverence for Scripture and for esoteric interpretations and hidden meanings taken from Scripture. If you can make bold claims for yourself and "prove" it from the Bible, you are on your way. But there is a price. Second Peter 3:16 says that certain people "wrest" the Scripture "unto their own destruction."

Why do people do this? Many, no doubt, are deliberately dishonest and will do anything to gain followers. Others, however, are responding out of some emotional trauma that is driving them with a zeal and earnestness that compels them to devote an unbelievable amount of effort to the perceived task ahead. They became zealous crusaders who are seeking to right a perceived wrong.

Teenagers often "lose their faith." All of us have heard stories of young people being brought up in church by godly Christian parents. As they advanced in years, however, there was a spirit of rebellion that grew stronger and stronger. They question everything about the Bible and about their faith and the faith of their parents. Sometimes they even move in with a same-sex partner.

We normally attribute this to science and its alleged conflict with Scripture, or to evil friends who are a bad influence. Supposedly they lose their faith because science has demonstrated that the Bible is in error and that no one can really believe the Bible in an age of modern science. But is this really the reason? The explanation lies in another direction. We lose more young people to some hurt than to science or friends. Their aberrant beliefs and practices are a way of lashing out and rectifying what they see as some evil or injustice. A dominant father, a cruel society, an overreaction by an authority figure— all contribute to a spirit of rebellion. That's why Scripture counsels, "Fathers, provoke not your children to anger, lest they be discouraged" (Col. 3:21).

If we are honest we will admit that homosexuals have often been traumatized by society and they are smarting from it—as if salt had been rubbed into a raw wound. In many cases their reinterpretation of Scripture is not so much a deliberate wresting of Scripture as it is an attempt to silence those whom they perceive to have caused them so much woe.

They find a deep satisfaction in using the same Bible used by traditionalists against them to silence those traditionalists. This does not excuse their behavior and mishandling of Scripture, but it helps to explain it. And, hopefully, it will help us to deal charitably with an aspect of the homosexual agenda that is often very troubling and that provokes us into reacting in an un-Christian manner. We all take a dim view of wresting Scripture. After all, who do they think they are?

The Account of Sodom and Gomorrah

Genesis 19 relates the doom of Sodom and Gomorrah. For centuries Jewish and Christian expositors have uniformly understood the sin of these cities to be homosexuality. Revisionists, however, take the sin of Sodom and Gomorrah to be inhospitality, homosexual rape, or perhaps even pride.

We will briefly exegete the passage and then make some comments and draw some conclusions from the text.

> And he [Lot] pressed upon them [the angelic visitors] greatly; and they turned in unto him, and entered into his house. . . .
>
> —Verse 3

The visitors did not want to be a burden on Lot and offered to stay in the town square, or some other public place. But, knowing that the homosexual population was on the prowl after hours, Lot insisted that the visitors spend the night inside with him.

> But before they lay down, the men of the city, even the men of Sodom, compassed the house round, both old and young, all the people from every quarter.
>
> —Verse 4

That these were men who wanted to "know" Lot's two visitors is repeated—"the men of the city, even the men of Sodom." If these men wanted just to check the visitors' passports why was the entire male population of the area involved, and not just the officials? This is a male mob, not the local authorities checking out passports.

After reading gay literature I was impressed with the number of older men who extol the virtues of homosexual sex. In fact, some of the leaders of the gay movement are older men. Interesting, isn't it, that this crowd included "both old and young" men?

> And they called unto Lot, and said unto him, Where are the men which came in to thee this night?
>
> —Verse 5

Their request was specific. They wanted "the men," i.e., the angels of verse one, who had come to stay with Lot. Lot was evidently unaware of the true identity of these men. For all intents and purposes they looked like men. Hebrews 13:2 counsels: "Be not forgetful to entertain strangers: for thereby some have entertained angels unawares."

> . . . bring them out unto us, that we may know them.

Their intent is clear. They didn't want to "know about" their passports, or where these men had come from, nor did they want to rob their billfolds. They wanted to "know" them.

"Know" (yada) can mean a knowledge of cognizance, i.e., "to know about," but it can mean much more. In verse eight Lot offers the men his daughters and he describes them by saying, "I have two daughters which have not known man." They were virgins and had not experienced sexual intimacy. If "know" means sexual intimacy in verse eight, why should we believe that it means something else in verse six?

> And Lot went out at the door unto them, and shut the door after him. . . .
>
> —Verse 6

Once again Lot is protecting his male guests. He goes outside to speak to the crowd, but shuts the door as an act of safety. That Lot sought to protect his guests once again suggests that he only knew them as men, not as superhuman angelic beings who would need no protection.

And said, I pray you, brethren, do not so wickedly.

—Verse 7

Lot knew that they intended something evil. It was a wicked thing that they were intending, hardly language that suggests checking out the passports of the visitors.

Behold now, I have two daughters which have not known man; let me, I pray you, bring them out unto you, and do ye to them as is good in your eyes: only unto these men do nothing; for therefore came they under the shadow of my roof.

—Verse 8

We are mystified that a father could offer his daughters to a crowd of men for their pleasure. Some argue that Middle Eastern hospitality was controlling Lot's actions. Lot indicated that they had come "under the shadow" of his roof. Verse three demonstrates Lot's deference for his guests. Even for the sake of his daughters' safety Lot, it is argued, would not violate the hospitality protocol. Others argue, however, that Lot knew that this crowd would reject female companionship since they were gay and therefore did not believe that his daughters were in any danger. These men were interested only in men.

Revisionists who claim to be history buffs argue that Lot was violating an ancient custom by entertaining guests without first getting the permission of the leaders of the city. They claim that by offering them his virgin daughters Lot was trying to avoid prosecution by bribing the crowd with two pretty girls. However, there is nothing in the account that even suggests this to be the case. The crowd is not angry with Lot for not having followed good protocol. In fact, the crowd is not much interested in Lot, but in his guests.

And they said, Stand back. And they said again, This one fellow came in to sojourn, and he will needs be a judge: now will we deal worse with thee, than with them.

—Verse 9

The gay crowd complains that Lot was judging their intended course of action. This certainly implies something evil on their part. These words sound so contemporary. Gay activists often complain that those who are opposed to their lifestyle are intolerant and judgmental. Contemporary activists are walking in the footsteps of their predecessors.

> And they pressed sore upon the man, even Lot, and came near to break the door.

This is the language of savage promiscuity. Some understand the sin of Sodom to be homosexual rape. It was not homosexuality that is condemned, but forcing oneself on a same-sex partner. But you can't separate an act of violence from the sin with which it is connected. If a man becomes violent while in the act of robbing a bank, this certainly does not mean that only the violence is wrong, and that if he robbed a bank peacefully and without violence the robbery would be legitimate.

> But the men [the angelic visitors] put forth their hand, and pulled Lot into the house to them, and shut the door.

—Verse 10

The visitors knew that Lot was in danger and that his attempts to deal rationally with this crowd were all to no avail.

> And they smote the men that were at the door of the house with blindness, both small and great: so that they wearied themselves to find the door.

—Verse 11

Another indication of the crazed lust of these men. Though they had been stricken with blindness they were still intent on committing the sin that had brought the blindness! Wouldn't the natural thing have been to admit their error and desist instead of rushing headlong to destruction?

Some argue that Sodom's sin was the rejection of these two strangers, which is inhospitality. No doubt, the men of Sodom were certainly not being hospitable. But Jesus references Sodom several times without ever identifying inhospitality as the characteristic sin of Sodom for which it was judged. Jesus compares several cities of his day with Sodom. If we examine Matthew 10:15, 11:23–24, and Mark 6:11, the explicit error of these cities was not the rejection of strangers—this is never even hinted at—but their rejection of the Good News of the Kingdom. Significantly this is the sin of many gays today. They reject the Gospel and the life-transforming power of Jesus Christ. Gays will not win the favor of God by being hospitable, but by repenting.

Homosexual Rape?

Lesbian author and Bible scholar Virginia Mollenkott argues that the sin of Sodom was not homosexuality, but homosexual rape. She is of the opinion that God approves of certain kinds of homosexual relationships but not forced relations. Mollenkott argues that what happened that night was much like prison rape, or the kind of sexual violence that would be committed by conquering armies.[4]

This argument seems plausible, but it assumes that the particular incident recorded in Genesis 19 is what precipitated divine judgment. God was angry at *this* crowd because of what *they* were intending to do.

However, Genesis 18:20 shows that God had already determined to destroy the city, even before what happened that particular night. The outcry of Sodom had already been heard by God. Even Abraham knew what God was about to do: "And Abraham drew near, and said, Wilt thou also destroy the righteous with the wicked?" (Gen. 18:23). It was the homosexual lifestyle that upset Lot. It was something that "vexed" Lot from "day to day" (2 Pet. 2:7–8).

Pride and a Lack of Compassion?

Revisionists point to Ezekiel 16:49 to show what Sodom's sin really was: "Behold, this was the iniquity of thy sister Sodom, pride, fulness of bread, and abundance of idleness was in her and in her daughters, neither did she strengthen the hand of the poor and needy." Revisionists are quick to point out that the sin of Sodom was pride and a lack of compassion. They were judged because of their lack of compassion for those who were needy.

I would agree that Sodom was carnally at ease. This carnality, which is symptomatic of a corrupted heart, demonstrates itself in many different kinds of sins. No doubt, Sodom's sin was not only homosexuality. However, this passage in Ezekiel does not rule out homosexuality. In fact, the following verse, verse 50 explains: "And they were haughty, and committed *abomination* before me"—language that aptly describes the homosexual sin of Sodom.

There are many sins in contemporary America. Turn on the nightly news and you will see what I mean. There is murder, rape, violence in the schools, child abuse, and many other criminal activities that are sinful activities. Every declining society has a number of ills that sap its moral vitality. Sodom and Gomorrah were no different. The homosexual revisionist argument based on Ezekiel 16:49 totally ignores this.

Leviticus Chapters 18 and 20

There are two important Scriptures in Leviticus that show God's attitude toward homosexuality.

- 18:22: "Thou shalt not lie with mankind, as with womankind: it is abomination."
- 20:13: "If a man also lie with mankind, as he lieth with a woman, both of them have committed an abomination: they shall surely be put to death; their blood shall be upon them."

These verses are clear in themselves, though they present some problems because of the death penalty prescribed. No conservative Christian that I know of argues that gays should be executed, just as none of us argues that rebellious children or adulterous women should be executed, as mandated in the Old Testament. Yet, such an admission does not mean that it is acceptable for children to rebel and for women to commit adultery. I am simply saying that the death penalty does not abrogate the entire teaching. The death penalty is abrogated, but the sin for which it was punishment has not ceased to be sin.

Homosexual revisionists will observe that the word "abomination," as found in these two passages, was a word that was invariably associated with idolatrous practices. The ancient Canaanites, they will argue, had idolatrous pagan rituals in which heterosexual and homosexual activities were a part of the religious service. Revisionist scholars will argue, therefore, that homosexuality was not really the problem but rather idolatry. It is homosexuality in connection with idolatry that is condemned because it was a violation of the Old Testament holiness code.

What shall we answer to this? We need to point out that Canaanite idolatry is only part of the picture. Yes, Leviticus deals with specific sins associated with the Canaanites and their possible influence on the ancient Israelites rather than the modern church in the twenty-first century. But it is also true that embedded in these chapters are a variety of sexual sins which are forbidden in the Old and New Testaments quite apart from the holiness code.

The association of a particular sin with ancient Israel does not mean that it is no longer a sin today. For example, in Ephesians 6:2–3 we read: "Honour thy father and mother; which is the first commandment with promise; That it may be well with thee, and thou mayest live long on the earth." Clearly, the promise of verse three—"that it may be well with thee, and thou mayest live long on the earth"—pertains to Israel. The Jewish people were promised a land. The church has no such promise. Yet, the moral requirement is unchanging. Children today are to honor their parents. By doing so they will enjoy long life. Avoiding strong drink, evil associations, and loose women will certainly prolong life.

Homosexuals believe that the prohibitions in Leviticus are prohibitions because of their associations with idolatry, but such is not true. They claim that the word "abomination" (to'evah) is associated with idolatry. While that is true in some of cases, there are other Scriptures where "abomination" has a broader application and describes violations of God's moral requirements: "These six things doth the LORD hate: yea, seven are an abomination [to'evah] unto him: A proud look, a lying tongue, and hands that shed innocent blood, An heart that deviseth wicked imaginations, feet that be swift in running to mischief, A false witness that speaketh lies, and he that soweth discord among brethren" (Prov. 6:16–19). These are described with the word "abomination," yet they are not restricted to the holiness code, nor are they conditioned on the idolatrous practices of the ancient Canaanites.

One other consideration is noteworthy, and that is the fact that Leviticus condemns a whole host of sexual aberrations in addition to homosexuality.

> None of you shall approach to any that is near of kin to him, to uncover their nakedness: I am the LORD. . . . The nakedness of thy sister, the daughter of thy father, or daughter of thy mother . . . their nakedness thou shalt not uncover. . . . Neither shalt thou lie with any beast to defile thyself therewith: neither shall any woman stand before a beast to lie down thereto: it is confusion"
>
> —Leviticus 18:6,9,23

The claim of the revisionists that the practices of Leviticus are condemned because of their associations with Canaanite idolatry leads to an important question. Would these practices be allowed if they were not connected with Canaanite idolatry? If so, then the sins listed in these chapters—some of the most vile imaginable—are all permissible as long as they are not performed in connection with the worship of a Canaanite deity. The absurdity of this needs no further comment.

Romans 1

One of the best known New Testament passages that has been used by traditionalists to condemn homosexuality is Romans 1:26–27:

> For this cause God gave them up unto vile affections: for even their women did change the natural use into that which is against nature: And likewise also the men, leaving the natural use of the woman, burned in their lust one toward another; men with men working that which is

unseemly, and receiving in themselves that recompence of their error which was meet.

This passage indicates that God sees lesbianism and homosexuality as one of the practices of fallen humanity. Fallen man is by nature a sinner and does that which is contrary to the will of God.

Homosexual Acts Committed by Heterosexuals?

A number of homosexual interpreters take exception with this interpretation. Paul, they argue, is not condemning homosexuals who commit homosexual acts. Rather, he is condemning heterosexuals who, contrary to their natural proclivities, engage in homosexual acts. It's God's condemnation of men and women engaging in unnatural homosexual behavior. This is what is "against nature."[5]

This interpretation is faulty, however, because it makes a distinction between homosexual acts committed by "true" homosexuals and homosexual acts committed by non-homosexuals. This is not a distinction found in the passage, but is cleverly brought in to allow the Bible to say something other than what it really says.

Romans 1 speaks about women who engage in sex acts with other women, and men who engage in sex acts with other men. It is women with women and men with men. This is what is condemned—not heterosexual women committing sex acts with women and heterosexual men committing sex acts with men. There is no suggestion that the Bible is condemning "what is not natural for me," but that it is condemning "what is not natural."

Moreover, the passages states that these men "burned in their lust one toward another." This does not describe a heterosexual man experimenting with something that he really has no interest in, or a heterosexual man engaging in unnatural homosexual acts for religious purposes. Rather it is describing one man lusting for another.

Other homosexual commentators, realizing that this argument is weak, claim that Paul is not speaking about homosexuality per se, but that Romans 1 is giving a blanket condemnation of idolatry. In Romans 1

Paul is speaking about idolatrous pagans, not about Christians who worship the true God. The pagans described here "changed the glory of the incorruptible God into an image made like to corruptible man, and to birds, and four footed beasts, and creeping things" (Rom. 1:23). "Yes," say the revisionists, "the acts described here in Romans 1 are wrong, but they are far different than the loving, homosexual relationships seen in today's world."

This is simply another evasion based on one aspect of what is in the text. Yes, Romans 1 speaks against idolatry, but there are other sins as well. When sin enters a society it takes many forms. In Romans 1:29–32, Paul cites at least twenty-two sins including fornication, envy, murder, hating God, disobeying parents, and so on. Are we to conclude that fornication is legitimate in God's sight as long as it is done in a loving way and not done by someone who is a murderer? Joe Dallas writes:

> Will the interpretation applied to verses 26–27 also apply to verses 29–30? Any sort of intellectual integrity demands it. If verses 26–27 apply to people who commit homosexual acts in connection with idolatry, and thus homosexual acts are not sinful if *not* committed in connection with idolatry, then the same must apply to verses 29–30 as well. Therefore we must assume that fornication, wickedness, covetousness, maliciousness, et al are also condemned by Paul *only* because they were committed by people involved in idolatry. . . . Which is, of course, ridiculous. Like homosexuality, these sins are not just born of idol worship; they are symptomatic of the fallen state. If we are to say homosexuality is legitimate, so long as it's not the result of idol worship, then we also have to say these other sins are legitimate as well, so long as they, too, are not practiced as a result of idolatry.[6]

Homosexual Acts with Minors

Some revisionists are quick to admit that Romans 1 condemns homosexual acts. They will argue, however, that Paul was not condemning all forms of homosexual relationships, but that he was only condemning pederasty. Pederasty, they claim, is the more dehumanizing form of homosexuality because it involves the manipulation of minors by adults for the pleasure of the adult.

Yet the passage says that homosexuals have left "the natural use of the woman" (Rom. 1:27). "The natural use of the woman" can only refer to *adult* male-female sexual relations. There is no suggestion here that adult male-female sexual relations have been abandoned for sexual relations between adults and children.

The latter words of verse twenty-seven bear this out. The apostle writes: ". . . men with *men* working that which is unseemly." He doesn't say "men with *boys* working that which is unseemly." The condemnation is clearly against homosexual activities, not only against restricted categories of homosexual activities.

"Against Nature"

Homosexual relations involve a changing of "the natural use into that which is against nature" (Rom. 1:26). The word "nature" (*phusis*) refers to the natural order, and to things as they are without the intervention of culture and social practice.

In Romans 2:27 Paul describes the "uncircumcision" as Gentiles "by nature," referring to those who are non-Jews. In Galatians 2:15 we read of those who are "Jews by nature." "Nature" refers to what Gentiles and Jews naturally are. By nature they are different.

In Romans 11:21,24 we read: "For if God spared not the natural branches [Jews who are by nature descendants of the patriarchal root], take heed lest he also spare not thee. . . . For if thou [the Roman Christians, Gentiles, not Jews, by nature] wert cut out of the olive tree which is wild by nature, and wert grafted contrary to nature into a good olive tree: how much more shall these, which be the natural branches, be grafted into their own olive tree?"

In Romans 11 the apostle is addressing the question of Israel. Has God forgotten, or canceled, His promises to Israel? If not, how come Israel is in a condition of unbelief, and how do Gentiles relate to Israel? The point Paul makes is that God still has a great future for Israel. Regarding Gentiles, they likewise are related to Israel and have been grafted contrary to nature into a Jewish tree.

Hence, by "nature" Paul is referring to the natural order, the order of creation. In no sense can something that is according to nature be considered a human invention, or a cultural development. In Romans 1 the apostle is arguing that homosexuality is contrary to the natural order as created by God. He does not mean that homosexuality violates "what is natural for me," but that it violates what is natural. As such, homosexuality is a violation of divine creation law.

This is an important consideration in view of the revisionist argument that the traditionalist opposition to homosexuality is cultural. No it's not. Homosexuality is a violation of the divine order. One cannot logically claim to believe that the divine order is normative and also embrace the homosexual lifestyle.

Further support for this is found in Paul's use of the word "change": "For even their women did change the natural use into that which is against nature." The apostle is defining "natural" as that which is natural according to the creation order. Homosexuality is a changing of this order and is therefore an attack on God's prerogative to define what is right. Homosexuality is an act of defiance. This is why the iniquity of Sodom is called "pride" by Ezekiel (Ezek. 16:49). The context of Romans 1:26–27 is one of human rebellion and arrogance against God. The apostle is simply articulating the consistent view of Scripture that homosexuality is a form of sinful pride and rebellion against the Creator and the order which He has established for His creatures.

This is explicit in the words "changing the truth of God" (Rom. 1:25). We have no right to change or alter that which God has expressly ordained. If you invite me to your house for dinner and I go around and start moving furniture and changing the décor, you would find me highly offensive. It's your house and I have no right redesigning it to suit my fancy. When homosexuals start "changing" God's design for human sexuality and then wresting Scripture to support that change, that is something that is highly offensive to God.

While homosexual sin is no worse than any other sin, the deliberate attempt to make it acceptable by putting words in God's mouth to make

Him say it is acceptable is an egregious example of human depravity and worthy of the harshest form of divine judgment. Homosexuals have been doing this for thousands of years. De Young writes: "According to Plato (*Laws* 636.d), the Cretans 'concocted' the story that their gods engaged in homosexual behavior. Does this have the modern parallel in the assertion by revisionists that Scripture does not oppose modern homosexuality?"[7]

1 Corinthians 6:9–11

This passage forms an important statement in the Bible regarding homosexuality. It is one of many forms of unrighteousness that, if not repented of, will exclude an individual from the Kingdom. The following brief exegesis of the passage shows both the seriousness of this as well as all sin, and affirms the ability of God to forgive and to cleanse. "Know ye not that the unrighteous shall not inherit the kingdom of God?" (vs. 9).

There is a complete incompatibility between unrighteousness and entry into the Kingdom. Because God is a moral being, He expects His children to bear the image of His righteousness. Salvation involves being remade into the image of God, something that has been greatly marred because of the fall. In the verses to follow the apostles describes "the unrighteous."

... Be not deceived ...

This is a warning. The tense of the verb suggests that these words could be translated as "stop deceiving yourselves." That Paul warns his readers not to deceive themselves suggests that some were being deceived. This gives these words a contemporary ring. People are being deceived today—even in the Church. "Feel-good" religion is not worth much. In fact, it is dangerous. It makes people complacent about their sins.

... neither fornicators ...

A fornicator is an unmarried person who enters into sexual relations with another person. This is much in style today. Contraceptives, "the pill," and rationalizations that "everybody is doing it," have spawned many fornicators.

. . . nor idolaters . . .

Those who follow false religions. Atheists fall into this category because rather than having no religion, they have the wrong one: the worship of self. Everybody has a source of authority and atheists are no exception. Some enshrine human reason, others speak about a general consensus of opinion. Idolatry is involved when individuals elevate their personal opinions and views above that which is revealed in the written Word of God.

. . . nor adulterers . . .

Married persons who violate their commitment to God and their spouse by being sexually involved with another individual. Adultery violates the clear commandment of God as well as the rights of the other partner.

. . . nor effeminate . . .

The word is *malakoi* and refers to men and boys who allow themselves to be abused by homosexuals, i.e., a passive homosexual partner.[8]

. . . nor abusers of themselves with mankind . . .

This is a translation of the word *arsenokoitai*. De Young states that "historical and cultural evidence supports the conclusion that the term must be broad enough to include both homosexual acts and the homosexual condition."[9]

De Young also states, "The evidence suggests that Paul coined the term, based on the juxtaposition of the two words *arsenos* and *koiten* in the LXX of Leviticus 20:13 (cf. similar phraseology in 18:22)."[10] The word is a compound made up of two words that had sexual connotations. *Koite* was used with reference to the marriage bed. It was also used in Romans 13:13 to refer to sexual excess. *Androkoites* specifically refers to a man who has a sexual relation with another man. It is possible that the reason Paul used *arsenokoitai* instead of *androkoitai* is because he was including a prohibition against pederasty. Paul took two words that were in common speech and joined them, much like the word "gayby" boomers.

Are there any clues in the text that help us to understand what Paul wanted to communicate to his readers? Evidently, 1 Corinthians was written to an audience that was familiar with Old Testament Judaism. The reference to Satan, the reference to being cut off, and the reference to the day of the Lord (1 Cor. 5:5) are indicative of this. There is also mention of "leaven" (vss. 6–8) and "passover" (vs. 7). Deuteronomy 17:7 is referenced in verse thirteen. Because Paul's Corinthian readers were obviously familiar with the Old Testament, De Young argues that *arsenokoitai* was specifically coined from Leviticus 20:13.[11]

The meaning of *arsenokoitai* is also confirmed by its connection with adultery. In 1 Corinthians 6:9-10 *arsenokoitai* and *malakoi* come after adultery. This is further evidence that *arsenokoitai* is a sexual sin. In 1 Timothy 1:10 *arsenokoitai* is connected with *pornois* ["fornicators"]. The *Greek-English Lexicon of the New Testament and Other Early Christian Literature* (Arndt and Gingrich) defines *arsenokoites* as "a male homosexual, pederast, sodomite" (p. 109). It is significant how the modern translations render *arsenokoitai*.

1 Corinthians 6:9—

> *The Living Bible*: "homosexuals"
> *The New International Version*: "homosexual offenders"
> *The New American Standard Version*: "homosexuals"
> *The New King James Version*: "sodomites"

1 Timothy 1:10—

> *The Living Bible*: "homosexuals"
> *The New International Version*: "perverts"
> *The New American Standard Bible*: "homosexuals"
> *The New King James Version*: "sodomites"

I am well aware of the limitations and shortcomings of these translations, but it is noteworthy that they seem to have no doubt that Paul is condemning homosexuality.

Not surprisingly, revisionists try to wiggle out of this evidence by saying that *arsenokoitai* only condemns homosexual prostitution but not loving homosexual relationships. Yet the only reason for this evasion is desperation. The words *arseno* ("male") and *koite* ("bed") do not imply prostitution. They simply imply a sexual activity, and it is one that God condemns.

The analogy with murder is helpful. God's Word condemns murder, whether it is done out of anger, or by a "hit man" who does it for hire. Murder is murder. Similarly, homosexuality is condemned in Scripture whether it is in the form of prostitution, or between two people who are doing it simply for their mutual enjoyment.

The passage closes with the words of 1 Corinthians 6:11 which are highly offensive to some homosexuals, but definitely an encouragement to those who want to do right: "And such were some of you." Homosexuality is a sin, but like all sin it can be forgiven and the homosexual can be spiritually made whole.

Jesus and Homosexuality

Recently a tract was circulating in some Episcopal congregations. It had these words on the cover: "What Jesus Said About Homosexuality." When the tract is opened, however, the reader is confronted with a blank page. The purpose of the tract is to demonstrate that if Jesus said nothing about something, and did not specifically forbid it, then the behavior must be permissible.

But how many verses can we find in our Bibles where Jesus specifically forbade wife-beating?

This approach is quite common with revisionists. It has a fatal flaw, however. It assumes that all of God's will is revealed in the words of Jesus. If something cannot be found in Matthew, Mark, Luke, or John, then it's really not a matter of concern to the Christian. But what did Jesus say about:

The ministry of the local church?
Spiritual gifts?
Marriage to a non-believer (see 1 Cor. 7:10)?
The doctrine of justification by faith alone?
Eating meat offered to idols?
Incest?

There are many things that are forbidden in other parts of the Bible, or that are addressed in other parts of the Bible, but not specifically dealt with by Jesus Christ. Are we to assume that if Jesus Christ did not address a topic it is not important?

Yes, Jesus did not directly address homosexuals, nor did He explicitly condemn homosexuality. But Jesus' words are not all that is communicated by Scripture.

Second Timothy 3:16 states: "All Scripture is given by inspiration of God and is profitable." Jesus' words only constitute *some* Scripture, not all of it. There is no biblical warrant to elevate the words of Jesus above other passages in the Bible. God did not give a red-letter edition of the Bible.

What Jesus Did Say

To say that Jesus said nothing about homosexuality is to build a straw house on the argument from silence—always risky business. While Jesus said nothing directly about homosexuality, He did say *much* about God's design for human sexuality. He did this by taking His audience back to the original creation order.

> And he answered and said unto them, Have ye not read, that he which made them at the beginning made them male and female, And said, For this cause shall man leave father and mother, and shall cleave to his wife: and they twain shall be one flesh? Wherefore they are no more twain, but one flesh. What therefore God hath joined together, let not man put asunder.
>
> —Matthew 19:4–6

The passage begins with the words, "And he answered." Jesus had been asked a question: "Is divorce within the will of God?" Instead of giving a simple "yes/no" answer, Jesus takes His audience back before the fall to God's original intent and design for marriage. Homosexuality is not mentioned at all. In establishing a monogamous relationship between one man and one woman as God's intent at creation, Jesus was condemning all other arrangements and possibilities.

Yes, Jesus said nothing specifically about homosexuality. But He did say much about legitimate sexual expression, and it is always in terms of relations between a husband and a wife.

There are a multitude of passages on marriage, divorce, child–rearing, church leaders and marriage, and other topics related to marriage. But in no passage of Scripture do we ever find any examples of lawful homosexual relationships. Contrast this silence with all of the Scriptures that teach about husbands and wives and you will see that the statement that "Jesus said nothing about homosexuality" sounds hollow and empty.

Jesus and the Law
In Matthew 5:17–18 we read: "Think not that I am come to destroy the law, or the prophets: I am not come to destroy, but to fulfil. For verily I say unto you, Till heaven and earth pass, one jot or one tittle shall in no wise pass from the law, till all be fulfilled."

The "jot" and "tittle" refer to the smallest minutia of the law. Specifically they signify the smallest parts of a Hebrew letter that distinguish one letter from another, as the curl of the "e" distinguishes it from a "c." Here, as well as in many other Scriptures, Jesus is affirming His relationship to the Old Testament law. He did not come to destroy the law but to fulfill all of its demands. It presents a righteousness that is totally in keeping with His ministry.

If Jesus endorsed homosexuality He would have been a hypocrite. The law condemned homosexuality. Jesus did not come to endorse that which God had earlier condemned. Jesus came into the world "made under the law" (Gal. 4:4).

The Episcopal tract that claims that Jesus said nothing about homosexuality and neither should we, is deliberately deceptive and manifestly erroneous.

CHAPTER 8

Redefining God

But there is forgiveness with thee, that thou mayest be feared.

—Psalm 130:4

O ne of the interesting things about the Word of God, the Bible, is that it presents a belief system that is totally unlike any conjured up by man. One of the remarkable aspects of God's revelation is that it teaches that divine forgiveness leads us to reverence God. Being forgiven by God does not make us presumptuous, or spiritually careless. Nor does it make us want to sin some more because we know God's grace will take care of the problem. Rather, in the words of the apostle, "Having therefore these promises, dearly beloved, let us cleanse ourselves from all filthiness of the flesh and spirit, perfecting holiness in the fear of God." Is that what revisionist theology teaches?

Revisionist theology teaches a false view of God, an erroneous view of divine love and forgiveness, and a completely unbiblical view of how the Christian views his or her duties to God. In short, revisionist theology redefines God.

This is one of the most serious consequences of revisionist theology. It not only destroys morality but completely destroys the biblical doctrine of sanctification and a true understanding of God which is vital to a proper understanding of the Christian life.

An Evolutionary Concept of God

We usually think of evolution as a way of explaining the origin of life apart from God. Evolution, however, is not simply restricted to the issue of origins. It is also a way of looking at God.

When the controversial Rev. Robinson was elevated to bishop in August of 2003 many applauded the Episcopal Church's leadership and praised a "Christianity which has come a long way and evolved with the times."

Most secular dictionaries have enough sense to define God as "perfect, omnipotent, the omniscient originator and ruler of the universe, the principal object of faith and worship in monotheistic religions." Even on the basis of this simple dictionary statement, any view of Christianity that says that it has evolved with the times could only be taken to mean that it has evolved into imperfection and is now a reflection of the sinful proclivities of its apostate leaders. As one writer put it, "The Episcopal Church's leadership have now chosen to spit in God's face. God allowed that once in the person of Jesus as He hung on that cross, in your place and mine. Those who reject His sacrifice and go their own way will endure God's righteous wrath firsthand for all of eternity."[1]

According to the clear teaching of Scripture, God is eternal and immutable. God has not evolved, is still intolerant of sin, and has not accepted political correctness as His method of judging behavior. A Christian is someone who loves what God loves and hates what God hates (see Rom. 12:9). God has made it abundantly clear in Scripture that homosexuality is sin and contrary to God's will. Yet homosexuality is now firmly establishing itself in some mainline denominations. Some were foolish to believe that homosexuality, which has firmly established itself in our culture, would not also work its way into the Church. It has and is an important end-time sign that the end of the present order is upon us.

There are at least two factors which have contributed to this flood of sin into churches. First, there has been a devaluation of the Bible.

Churches are becoming more and more intent on entertaining their congregations instead of teaching God's Word. Entertained Christians are suckers for accepting falsehood as truth. Secondly, there has been a redefining of tolerance and an elevation of this new view of tolerance into a supreme virtue.

At one time tolerance meant tolerating those things that you do not agree with. Tolerance was not intended to indicate approval, but something that simply grew out of the recognition of the fact that in a large pluralistic society there are some things that we cannot change and have to live with. In some measure we tolerate air pollution, traffic congestion, and increases in utility bills, but we don't approve of those things. The new view of tolerance, however, is based on the faulty view that one person's belief is just as legitimate as another's and that standards of behavior are what we make them to be.

Such a view of tolerance is restricted to religious and moral issues. "Our boss won't tolerate it if we come to work at 9:30 when we were supposed to be there at 8:00," notes Christian commentator Janet Parshall. "So when did we decide that tolerance was a transcendent ethic?" she asks.[2]

Those who seek to make tolerance a transcendent ethic vilify Christians as the purveyors of hate and intolerance. Called "homophobes," Christians are treated as a scourge that is pulling society back into some ignorant past, when passion instead of reason ruled the day. Christians are regarded as being against human values.

Interestingly, however, Bible-believing Christians have been on the forefront of civil rights and race issues, and have been outspoken critics of slavery. Moreover, Christians have seen many homosexual lives transformed by the grace of God. They offer life-changing power through the Gospel. Though Christians are maligned as creating an atmosphere of hate which contributes to violence, it is only faulty logic that makes such a claim. Should a poster that reminds people of the danger of smoking be construed as creating an atmosphere of hate against smokers and those who raise tobacco?

How tolerant are those who seek to inculcate tolerance? Four Christians were recently kicked out of Veterans Stadium during the Philadelphia Phillies' "Gay Community Day." They brought a banner to the ballpark that read: "Homosexuality is sin. Christ can set you free."

Seven minutes after unfurling their banner from their centerfield seats the group was approached by security. They were told that they could not display that banner. While several other banners were permitted in the park that day, including a large rainbow flag sported by a homosexual, the Christians challenged the singling out of their group. They were told "it's the content of the message" that is offensive.[3]

"I'm Gay and It's Okay"

One doesn't have to read very far in the voluminous amount of material turned out by revisionists before one is confronted with the statement: "Yes, I'm gay, but I'm also a Christian. Jesus died for me and He loves me."

What is the intent of a statement like this? Simply to show that God approves of the gay lifestyle. "I'm gay and God has accepted me. Being gay, therefore, must be okay."

This argument is absurd. It says, in effect, "I'm saved and whatever I do is okay." But is it? People who are bank robbers and who cheat on their income tax and who engage in binge drinking could very well profess salvation, but God approves of none of these activities. God doesn't save people so that He could become like them. Rather He saves people so that they could become like Him (1 John 2:6).

While this is not the place to engage in a discussion of whether or not eternal security is taught in the Bible, the fact is that Christians do sin. God's ideal is that we do not sin. But that's not all that's said in Scripture. "And if any man sin, we have an advocate with the Father, Jesus Christ the righteous" (1 John 2:1).

This verse, and others like it, presuppose that Christians often sin and need to confess their sins. Salvation does not legitimize sin, even those sins that are committed by a child of God. In God's sight sin is sin, whether committed by a believer or a non-believer. Being a Christian is no guarantee that one's life will be totally pleasing to God. No matter how certain an individual is that he or she is walking in conformity to God's will, that person may be totally deceived. Deception is often the product of unbridled lusts that wage war against the mind and spirit. This is exactly what the Bible says about those who engage in homosexual sin. They became "vain in their imaginations, and their foolish heart was darkened. Professing themselves to be wise, they became fools" (Rom. 1:21–22).

"... And the Gifts Are In Evidence"

There is a variation of the above argument. Some homosexuals will state that they are gay, along with other church members, and all the gifts of the Spirit are in evidence and therefore homosexuality must have God's approval.

This, like the other argument, is also weak. The church at Corinth evidently had individuals in the fellowship who were gifted, but it was also a problem church. The presence of spiritual gifts does not necessarily indicate that God approves of everyone and everything in the fellowship.

Some of the brethren in Corinth were "carnal" and the church was riddled with division (1 Cor. 3). There was a man who was engaged in an incestuous relationship (1 Cor. 5) and the saints were taking each other to court and holding Christ up to ridicule (1 Cor. 6). Furthermore, there were some in the fellowship who denied one of the cardinal doctrines of the Christian faith, the resurrection (1 Cor. 15).

While some would be inclined to argue that perhaps the gifts were really not in evidence in the Corinthian church and that the spiritual experiences being claimed were really satanic counterfeits, we need not enter into a discussion of that for the purpose at hand. Deception is always a possibility. However, one only has to note that the presence of the Holy Spirit in a fellowship does not necessarily indicate divine approval of all that goes on there. Remember, the presence of God is a sign of grace, not approval.[4]

It is entirely possible that some of the gifts are in evidence in a fellowship even though there are professing Christians who are not living in perfect conformity with the will of God. The church is a hospital for sinners and hospitals need doctors. However, doctors are in hospitals for the purpose of healing, not for the purpose of keeping people sick.

Even though God's love is unconditional, and we likewise are to love unconditionally, this only means that we must accept the person, not the sin. We are to love racists, but we do not accept their racism. Nowhere in the Bible are we told unconditional love means accepting the sinner and the sin.

The story is sometimes told of the little boy who was raised in the country. When the boy and his friends played baseball, they used a cow paddy as home plate. One day, after the little boy slid into home plate, he brought victory to his team. He went home to tell his mother about his home run. She said, "Son, I accept your person, but not your condition." She loved her son unconditionally, but before he could sit at the dinner table he needed a bath.

Should we be silent or should we confront what many misguided individuals believe to be right and proper and good? Doesn't love accept anything and everything? Not according to the Bible.

> Now we command you, brethren, in the name of our Lord Jesus Christ, that ye withdraw yourselves form every brother that walketh disorderly, and not after the tradition which ye received of us. . . . And if any man obey not our word by this epistle, note that man, and have no company with him, that he may be ashamed. Yet count him not as an enemy, but admonish him as a brother.
>
> —2 Thess. 3:6,14–15

The simple truth is that God who is love does not accept every behavior. If He were accepting of every behavior He could not be love. God's love is discriminating. He desires the best for His people, which comes from conformity to the will of God, not from rebellion against it. When Paul heard of gross immorality in the Corinthian assembly (incest with a step-mother) he ordered the man to be removed from the fellowship. Why? Because "a little leaven leaveneth the whole lump" (1 Cor. 5:6). Homosexual activists want to criminalize church discipline, and legislate against it under the category of "hate crimes."

Judgment, Discernment, and Love

In a web article entitled "Homosexuality: Not a Sin, Not a Sickness" we read a pretty typical statement about the transcendent nature of love.

> The rarity with which Paul discusses any form of same-sex behavior and the ambiguity in references attributed to him make it extremely unsound to conclude any sure position in the New Testament on homosexuality, especially in the context of loving, responsible relationships. Since any arguments must be made from silence, it is much more reliable to turn to great principles of the Gospel taught by Jesus Christ and the apostles. Love God with all your heart, and love your neighbor as yourself. Do not judge others, lest you be judged. The fruit of the Holy Spirit is love . . . against such there is no law.[5]

I have shown that the Bible is not ambiguous in what it says about homosexuality. But what about the statement, "Do not judge others, lest you be judged"? My answer: The Bible *never* says that.

Matthew 7:1 is often used to teach that we should not judge. It states: "Judge not, that ye be not judged." However, a text without a context is a pretext. Verse two and following makes it very clear that we are not to exercise hypocritical judgment. We are to judge others in the same way that we want to be judged: honestly and fairly. In verses three through five Jesus says: "And why beholdest thou the mote ["speck"] that is in thy brother's eye, but considerest not the beam that is in thine own eye? Or how wilt thou say to thy brother, Let me pull out the mote out of thine eye; and, behold, a beam is in thine own eye? Thou hypocrite, first cast out the beam out of thine own eye; and then shalt thou see clearly to cast out the mote out of thy brother's eye."

Significantly, later in the chapter Jesus tells His disciples that judgment is necessary: "Beware of false prophets, which come to you in sheep's clothing, but inwardly they are ravening wolves." The idea is that you do not always get what you see. You have to be discerning, and you do that by exercising judgment.

Scripture relates that King Solomon "loved" many wives, but they turned his heart away from God (1 Kings 11:3–4). Love didn't lead him to glorify God. Rather, it became a snare and a stumbling block and led Solomon to dishonor God. Don't worship love. While the Bible says, "God is love" (1 John 4:8), it never says "Love is God." How could it? That would be idolatry!

CHAPTER 9

Remodeling Behavior

There is a way that seemeth right unto a man, but the end thereof are the ways of death.

—Proverbs 16:25

Moral values determine what is considered moral behavior. When moral values are changed our estimate of what is moral behavior also changes. *If* moral values are simply a reflection of what we are, then behavior that is innate and natural cannot be considered immoral. Just as a white man cannot be considered morally culpable for being white, neither can a homosexual be considered sinful because he engages in homosexual activities. It is just part of his nature, which is neither good nor bad.

New and amazing advances in genetics, microbiology, and biochemistry have fueled speculation that homosexuality is simply a reflection of what some people are by virtue of their underlying makeup. This concept is gaining in popularity. Man is no longer a sinner but simply a victim. The idea of moral accountability, therefore, is illogical. With thinking like this growing in popularity, it is quite proper to say that civilization is on the doorstep of a new and radical biological determinism. Our lives are determined not by our choices but by our nature. Our choices are simply a reflection of what we are.

This belief is seen in a comment that is frequently made by homosexuals: "As long as I can remember I've been gay." This is intended to end all discussion. But this certainly does not mean that homosexuality is genetic, innate, or biologically determined. As Dailey observes, there are a number of social and environmental factors contributing to why people find themselves attracted at an early age to other people of the same sex.[1]

The Quest for the Biological Origin of Homosexuality

In the last decade of the twentieth century several supposedly scientific studies were advanced to demonstrate that homosexuals are that way not by choice but by nature. Since homosexuality is natural for some people, it can't be wrong.

One of the first such studies was advanced by a Dr. Simon LeVay, a neuroscientist at the Salk Institute of La Jolla, California, allegedly showing a connection between homosexuality and the hypothalamus. In 1991 Le Vay examined the brains of forty-one cadavers, nineteen of whom were supposedly homosexual men, and sixteen who were supposedly heterosexual men, and six women who claimed to be heterosexual.

LeVay's research focused on a group of neurons in the hypothalamus called the interstitial nuclei of the anterior hypothalamus, or the INAH3. LeVay concluded that homosexuality is innate and is caused by size variations in the INAH3. This conclusion has been widely hailed by homosexuals because, if true, it shows that homosexuality is no more right, nor wrong, than blue eyes or blonde hair.

Though hailed by homosexuals and liberals as a great discovery, LeVay's conclusions have been widely challenged by experts in science. Many of LeVay's peers in the field of neuroscience have cited several weaknesses in both LeVay's methodology and conclusions. Should the INAH3, for example, be measured by size/volume or by the number of neurons? Moreover, one of LeVay's colleagues at the Salk Institute said that it is not clear whether brain structure affects behavior or whether behavior affects brain structure. If the latter is true, any unique characteristics in the INAH3s of homosexuals could simply be the *result* of their homosexuality and not the *cause* of it.[2]

Another 1991 study that supposedly showed some kind of innate basis for homosexuality was a study done by psychologist Michael Bailey of Northwestern University and psychiatrist Richard Pillard of Boston University School of Medicine. They excitedly announced their findings that, among the identical twins studied, 52 percent were both homosexual as opposed to fraternal twins among whom only 22 percent shared a homosexual orientation.

Interestingly, however, Pillard and Bailey's findings actually show that there is something more than genes that affects sexual orientation. If almost half (48 percent) of identical twins do NOT share the same sexual orientation then there is something more than genetics alone which is causing and directing sexual orientation. It would appear that environment was also playing a significant role in determining sexual orientation.

A second problem comes from the twins studied. They were all raised in the same households. The 52 percent of identical twins that were homosexual may simply have been influenced by their environment. If these identical twins had been raised in a *different* environment then we might conclude that homosexuality is influenced by something innate. But because of the way the study was conducted, such a conclusion cannot be reached.

A third problem is that in 1992 the *British Journal of Psychiatry* tried to replicate Pillard and Bailey's experiment but got completely different results. It reported that only 20 percent of the homosexual twins in the study had a gay co-twin, leading the researchers to conclude that "genetic factors are insufficient as an explanation of the development of sexual orientation."[3]

Science magazine for July 1993 featured an article by molecular geneticist Dean Hamer that was purported to have found a genetic cause for homosexuality. National Public Radio, the *Wall Street Journal,* the *New York Times,* and other media outlets announced: "Report Suggests Homosexuality Is Linked to Genes." Though the necessary disclaimers were liberally sprinkled through the Hamer report, most people had concluded from reading the report that there is a genetic basis to homosexuality and that such is an indisputable scientific conclusion.

How valid are the conclusions reached by the Hamer report? Jeffrey Satinover, M.D., who is a former Fellow in Psychiatry and Child Psychiatry at Yale University, finds many problems with the Hamer study.

> Even though a trait may have a chromosomal link, it does not necessarily mean it is genetic. Genetic traits are those, such as eye colors, that are coded for us by genes alone. . . . Behavioral traits, such as weight, are influenced by genetics, but unlike genetic traits, most behavioral traits are programmed by multiple genes and things such as the environment in the womb, the mother's health habits, or postnatal effects of a virus. Behavioral traits, as opposed to simple, single-gene physiological traits such as eye color, always interact in this way.
>
> Demonstrating that any behavioral state is not only biological but genetic is well beyond our present research capacity. This is especially true for something so complex and nuanced as homosexuality. One psychiatric researcher, Brian Suarez, calculated that at least 8,000 people would be required for a study to confirm a behavioral trait as genetic. No study of homosexuality has come remotely close to these requirements.[4]

Satinover observes that genetics researchers from Yale, Columbia, and Louisiana State Universities have all noted that there are many irregularities with the Hamer study and the methodology used to arrive at the announced conclusions. "They also indicated that the results were not consistent with any genetic model and should be interpreted cautiously." Satinover makes the following telling comment regarding the so-called "gay gene" by saying, "In other words, any claims to have found a 'gay gene' were overblown if not outright wrong."[5]

So What?

Even if it could be demonstrated that there is a homosexual gene, I would have to ask: "So what?" A number of birth defects have been studied at length. Some affect speech, thinking, physical abilities, and other aspects of the individual's life. They sometimes have genetic and biochemical causes, but this does not mean that they are "normal," "good," "desirable," or even "neutral." Certain studies have shown that some cancers have a genetic basis, yet this does not make cancer "good."

A number of studies suggest that there may be genetic causes that influence the development of alcoholism, violent behavior, obesity, and even marital infidelity, as reported by *Time* magazine (August 15, 1994), yet are we to conclude that these behaviors are acceptable? As former homosexual activist and staff member of the gay Metropolitan Community Church, Joe Dallas, has stated: "Immoral behavior cannot be legitimized by a quick baptism in the gene pool."[6]

The implications of finding a supposed genetic basis for any kind of behavior are often misunderstood. The purpose on which the claims for a "gay gene" rests is the unreasonable assumption that if a behavior is genetic it must be legitimate and should achieve some legitimacy and protection under the law. But supposing a "murder gene" or "rape gene" is discovered? Does this somehow legitimize murder and rape? Does this mean that murderers and rapists should now have some kind of equal protection under the law? Would the politically correct thing be to make sure that men who have the "rape gene" be employed in women's hospitals?

While some find it significant that homosexuality may be inborn, such a possibility is no surprise to the Christian. The human race is a fallen race. Our natures are corrupt and we all have a tendency to evil. This tendency is not something that is produced by our environment. Rather, we are "by nature" children of wrath (Eph. 2:3). It is foolhardy to assume that because we bring a certain behavior from the womb to life that therefore that behavior is divinely-sanctioned by God.

While there is no compelling proof that homosexuality is genetic, biological, or innate, it doesn't really matter if there were. If it could be demonstrated that destructive behavior is innate, that does not justify destructive behavior nor make it acceptable. Should we now create a new category of anti-discrimination laws because some smokers claim they can't break the habit and therefore need protection against overzealous people who insist on living in a smoke-free environment?

Toward the close of his book *Homosexuality and the Politics of Truth,* Jeffrey Satinover, M.D., gives several concluding propositions:

- Each individual's homosexuality is the likely result of a complex mixture of genetic, intrauterine, and extrauterine biological factors combined with familial and social factors as well as repeatedly reinforced choices. These create a particular blend of impulses. The role of genetic influence is small, and in any event means very little in terms of compelling an individual to become homosexual.
- Homosexual behavior is difficult to modify because, like other forms of compulsive behavior, it involves innate impulses and reinforced choices by which sinful activities become embedded in the brain ("engraved on the heart").
- Ethical demands require homosexuals, like all people, to resist their natural sinful impulses.
- Homosexuality is not a true illness, though it may be thought an illness in the spiritual sense of "soul sickness," innate to fallen human nature. Its treatment thus opens directly into the domain of the "cure of souls."
- Because deeply engraved behaviors are so difficult to modify, homosexuals, like all people, have two choices: to capitulate to the behavior and its consequences or to depend on others, and on God, for help.
- The modern change in opinion concerning homosexuality, though presented as a scientific advance, is contradicted rather than supported by science. It is a transformation in public morals consistent with widespread abandonment of the Judeo-Christian ethic upon which our civilization is based. Though

hailed as "progress," it is really a reversion to ancient pagan practices supported by a modern restatement of gnostic moral relativism.[7]

The Judeo-Christian Scriptures acknowledge that sinful people do sinful things. Yet these same Scriptures call on us to deny evil impulses, not to capitulate to them or glorify them. Christian medical doctor Jeffrey Satinover reminds us that "monotheistic worship leads away from the violent, hedonistic, and orgiastic. Because instincts are creaturely and not divine, they must not be elevated as final arbiters of individual and social mores. In other words, instincts are not to be worshipped."[8]

Are All Same-Sex Friendships Blemished with Lust?

One of the sad consequences of all the media coverage given to this issue is that all same-sex relationships are naturally thought of as homosexual relationships. The relationship between David and Jonathan is an example. Certain passages are singled out by activists to make their case:

- 1 Samuel 18:1: "And it came to pass, when he had made an end of speaking unto Saul, that the soul of Jonathan was knit with the soul of David, and Jonathan loved him as his own soul."
- 1 Samuel 19:2: "But Jonathan Saul's son delighted much in David."
- 1 Samuel 20:41: "David arose out of a place toward the south, and fell on his face to the ground, and bowed himself three times: and they kissed one another, and wept one with another."
- 2 Samuel 1:26: "I am distressed for thee, my brother Jonathan: very pleasant hast thou been unto me: thy love to me was wonderful, passing the love of women."

The words "loved" and "kissed" lead activists to read all kinds of things into the relationship between David and Jonathan that are not there.

Some would argue that their relationship is a prototype of homosexual unions in the present time. It's a shame that such innocent passages are packed with so much meaning by those who seek to justify their lifestyles! Titus 1:15 describes it quite well: "Unto the pure all things are pure: but unto them that are defiled and unbelieving is nothing pure; but even their mind and conscience is defiled."

There are at least three important considerations to keep in mind when dealing with these passages and those who find homoerotic activities implicit in them.

1. There is never any indication that the relationship between David and Jonathan was erotic, nor are there any erotic scenes described in connection with David and Jonathan.

   There are erotic scenes in the Bible, some being quite explicit, as in the Song of Solomon, which the ancient rabbis kept from Jewish men who were under twenty-one years of age; or the scene in which Potiphar's wife invites Joseph with the words, "Lie with me" (Gen. 39:7). Ruth 4:13 is also explicit: "So Boaz took Ruth, and she was his wife: and when he went in unto her, the LORD gave her conception, and she bare a son." When the Bible wants to speak about sex it does. But it never even intimates that there was anything sexual in the relationship between David and Jonathan.

2. Homosexual revisionists equate love between two men with sex between two men. The word "love," however, has a wide variety of meanings and connotations. To deny the possibility of non-sexual intimacy between friends of the same sex is to virtually deny the profound depths of true friendship. "To inject a sexual component into any loving human relationship outside of marriage—including those between parents and children, siblings, as well as friendships—would be both morally wrong and destructive."[9]

3. The original language words used in the Hebrew text do not indicate sexual intimacy between David and Jonathan. When

1 Samuel 18:1 says that their souls were "knit together," this language explicitly precludes erotic activity. It does not say that they became "one flesh." They were "soul mates," not "bed mates."

4. In the ancient Near East men kissed the way they shake hands in the present day. It was a form of greeting and a way of departing. The apostle often addressed the churches and said, "Salute ["greet"] one another with an holy kiss" (Rom. 16:16). When Paul departed from the Ephesian elders, they were heartbroken because they had some intimation that they might never see Paul again in this life. "And they all wept sore, and fell on Paul's neck, and kissed him" (Acts 20:37). If all of these passages were eroticized simply because they convey expressions of love, we would surely get the wrong idea of the depth of close human relationships.

The Mandate Is Still Unconditional Love

But God commendeth his love toward us, in that, while we were yet sinners, Christ died for us.

—Romans 5:8

Irrespective of what gay lobbyists are trying to do, God does love the sinner but hates the sin. A holy God hates sin. There is simply no other way to put it. Yet it is also true that God loves people, and wants the best for them—and the homosexual lifestyle is not the best for anyone.

While the homosexual lifestyle is contrary to God's best, it is also true that Christians need to speak the truth in love (Eph. 4:15). Sometimes, however, we have failed miserably in this.

As Christians, we've too often been quick to judge those who are caught up in a lifestyle that is alien to us. It is hard for us to understand why they persist in living the way they do. We've written articles, preached sermons, and some of us have even held up signs stating: "God Hates Fags." Surely, when we see the insensitive way homosexuals have often been treated, it is no mystery why they think that Christians are cruel and uncaring.

In confronting sin, the proper attitude is essential. First Peter 3:15 states: "Be ready always to give an answer to every man that asketh you a reason of the hope that is in you *with meekness and fear.*" Homosexuals are sinners. We, too, are sinners. Being a heterosexual does not immediately put a person in a state of grace. The wrong kinds of heterosexual desires are also categorized as "sin."

Andrew Aquino of the Columbus Baptist Association put it this way: "My message to the homosexual is: We love you. Come and struggle with us against sin. Don't give in to it."[1]

End Notes

Introduction

1. William Norman Grigg, "Unmentionable Vice Goes Mainstream," *The New American,* November 18, 2002, p. 8.
2. Timothy J. Dailey, *Dark Obsession: The Tragedy and Threat of the Homosexual Lifestyle* (Nashville: Broadman and Holman, 2003), p. 37.

Chapter 1

1. "The War Over Gay Marriage," (*Newsweek,* July 7, 2003), pp. 42–43.
2. Jeffrey Satinover, *Homosexuality and the Politics of Truth* (Grand Rapids, MI: Baker, 1996), p. 32.
3. Ibid.
4. Satinover, p. 33.
5. Ibid., p. 34.
6. Joe Dallas, "Responding to Pro-Gay Theology" (*www.leaderu.com/jhs/dallas.html,* August 7, 2003.
7. David French, *A Season for Justice* (Nashville: Broadman and Holman, 2002), p. 66.
8. William Norman Grigg, "Reigning Supreme," *The New American,* July 28, 2003), p. 10.
9. James B. De Young, *Homosexuality: Contemporary Claims Examined in Light of the Bible and Other Ancient Literature and Law* (Grand Rapids: Kregel, 2000), p. 37.
10. Ibid., p. 261.
11. Ibid., p. 261.
12. Ibid., p. 237.

13. Ibid., p. 73.

14. Timothy J. Dailey, *Dark Obsession: The Tragedy and Threat of the Homosexual Lifestyle* (Nashville: Broadman & Holman, 2003), p. 104.

15. Alan Sears and Craig Osten, *The Homosexual Agenda: Exposing the Principal Threat to Religious Freedom Today* (Nashville: Broadman and Holman, 2003), p. 14.

Chapter 2

1. Barbara Curtis, "(Gay) School Days," *www.family.org,* July 31, 2003.

2. French, p. 49.

3. Ibid., p. 48.

4. Curtis.

5. Stanley Monteith, *AIDS: The Unnecessary Epidemic* (Sevierville, TN: Covenant House Books, 1991), pp. 104–105.

6. Christina Hoff Sommers, *The War Against Boys: How Misguided Feminism Is Hurting Our Young Men* (New York: Simon and Shuster, 2000), p. 194.

7. David Thorstad, "Pederasty and Homosexuality," *www.namblal.de/pederasty.htm,* August 26, 2002, p. 8.

8. Steve Brown, "Fears Grow Over Academic Efforts to Normalize Pedophilia," *www.cnsnews.com,* July 10, 2003.

9. Ibid.

10. "Harry Hay and the Spirit of Stonewall—New York 1994," *www.namblal.desosconference1994.htm,* August 26, 2003.

11. Thorstad, "Pederasty and Homosexuality," p. 2.

12. "Harry Hay and the Spirit of Stonewall."

13. Dailey, p. 114.

14. Ibid., p. 116.

15. Timothy J. Dailey, "Homosexuality and Child Sexual Abuse," *www.frc.org/get//ifo2g2.cfm,* August 27, 2003.

16. Ibid.

17. George Grant and Mark A. Horne, *Legislating Immorality* (Franklin, TN: Moody Press/Legacy Communications, 1993), p. 41.

18. "Exposed: Homosexual Child Molesters," *www.traditionalvalues.org/urban/one.php,* August 27, 2003.

19. Grant and Horne, pp. 40–41.

20. "What Does Science Have To Say? Debunking the Myths About Man/Boy Love," *www.namblal.de/benefit.htm,* August 26, 2003.

21. Eli Shuster, "Study shows link between homosexuality and Pedophilia," *www.lifesite.net/interim/2002/Sept/02Study.html,* August 27, 2003.

22. Timothy J. Dailey, "Homosexuality and Child Sexual Abuse."

23. Grant and Horne, p. 39.

Chapter 3

1. Grant and Horne, p. 46.

2. Grant and Horne, pp. 44–45.

3. Jan LaRue, "Why Homosexual 'Marriage' Is Wrong," *www.cwfa.org,* September 26, 2003.

4. Ibid.

5. Ed Vitagliano, "Unholy Matrimony. Should 'Gays' Be Allowed To Marry?" *www.headlines.agapepress.org,* August 28, 2003.

6. Dailey, *Dark Obsession,* p. 97.

7. Vitagliano.

8. Dailey, *Dark Obsession,* p. 106.

9. Ibid., p. 107.

10. Terry Phillips, "Texas Case Spotlights 'Gay-on-Gay' Domestic Violence," *www.family.org,* July 4, 2003.

11. Michael Foust, "Presidential Candidates Supporting 'Civil Unions,'" *SBC Life,* September 2003, p. 10.

12. "The War Over Gay Marriage," p. 40.

13. Grigg, "Reigning Supreme," p. 10.

14. Ibid., p. 11.

15. "Gay Pride Parades Celebrate Supreme Court Ruling," *www.foxnews.com,* June 30, 2003.

16. Lisa Leff, "Gays Praise Court Ruling on Sodomy," *www.apnews1.iwon,* June 30, 2003.

17. Frank J. Murray, "Obscenity law in Ohio targeted by lawyer," *www.washtimes.com,* July 23, 2003.

18. Ibid.

19. David Horowitz, *The Art of Political War* (Dallas: Spence Publishing, 2000), x.

20. Ibid., xi.

21. William Norman Grigg, "Internationalizing the Court," *The New American,* July 28, 2003, p. 13.

22. George Neumayr, "Sodomy in the Age of Oprah," *www.spectator.org,* July 4, 2003.

23. Grigg, "Internationalizing the Court," p. 13.

24. Ibid.

25. Ibid

26. Alan E. Sears, "Foreign Jurisprudence Must Not Apply Here,"

www.pointofview.net/ar_jurisprudence.htm, September 5, 2003.

27. Grigg, "Reigning Supreme," p. 12.

28. Sears and Osten, p. 191.

29. Leff, "Gays Praise Court Ruling."

Chapter 4

1. Grant and Horne, p. 99.

2. "Position Statement: Hate Crimes Laws—Focus on the Family," *www.family.org.,* July 3, 2003.

3. French, pp. 70–71.

4. Sears and Osten, p. 185.

5. Ibid., p. 184.

6. Grigg, "Unmentionable Vice Goes Mainstream," p. 8.

7. Sears and Osten, p. 188.

8. Ibid., pp. 192–193.

9. Jim Brown and Chad Groening, "School Regulation Punishes 'Discrimination Against Homosexuals,'" *www.agapepress.org,* July 3, 2003.

10. French, p. 165.

11. Sears and Osten, p. 174.

12. Ibid.

13. Ibid. pp. 176–177.

14. Dailey, *Dark Obsession,* p. 128.

15. Grant and Horne, p. 52.

16. Ibid. pp. 52–53.

17. Sears and Osten, p. 205.

18. Tammi Reed Ledbetter, "Salt and Light for a Decaying and Dark World," *SBC Life,* September 2003, p. 1.

19. Ibid.

20. Monteith, p. 250.

Chapter 5

1. Joseph Nicolosi, "Why Reveal the Dark Side of the Gay Movement?" *www.narth.com/docs/whyreveal.htmls,* August 27, 2003.

2. "Homosexual Behavior Fuels AIDS and STD Epidemic," *www.traditional-values.org,* August 27, 03).

3. Ibid.

4. Ibid.

5. Grant and Horne, p. 35.

6. Ibid., p. 37.

7. Satinover, pp. 49–51.

8. Monteith, pp. 57–58.

9. Ibid., p. 60.

10. Ibid., p. 61.

11. Grant and Horne, pp. 127–128.

12. Monteith, p. 96.

13. Ibid., p. 105.

14. Mychal Massie, "If health costs are key, why not sue sodomists?" *wnd.com/ news/article.asp?ARTICLE_ID=34168,* August 22, 2003.

15. Monteith, p. 57.

Chapter 6

1. Grigg, "Unmentionable Vice," p. 8.

2. Dailey, *Dark Obsession,* p. 108.

3. Sears and Osten, p. 74.

4. Ben Shapiro, "Militant gay English on the rise," *www.townhall.com/columnists/ benshapiro/bs20030820.shtml,* August 21, 2003.

5. Sears and Osten, p. 76.

6. Ibid.

7. Ibid., p. 77.

8. Goldberg, *Bias,* p. 76.

9. Ibid., pp. 76–77.

10. "Jesse Dirkhising Was Murdered by Joshua Brown and Davis Carpenter," *www.tajj.com/jessedirkhising/index.html,* August 7, 2003.

11. Mackubin Thomas Owens," Gays don't belong in military," *www.dadi.org/ nogaygis.htm,* September 1, 2003.

12. Ibid.

13. Ibid.

14. Ibid.

15. Grant and Horne, p. 153.

16. Ibid., p. 148.

Chapter 7

1. Al Dobras, "Oxford's New Pro-Homosexual Bible A Hit With Gay Activists," *www.cultureandfamily.org,* September 15, 2002.

2. Joe Dallas, p. 33.

3. Ibid., pp. 32–33.

4. Ibid., p. 26.

5. Ibid., p. 29.

6. Ibid., p. 31.

7. DeYoung, p. 262

8. De Young, pp. 154, 196.

9. Ibid., p. 194.

10. Ibid., p. 195.

11. Ibid., p. 198.

Chapter 8

1. Craige McMillan, "Laodicean Episcopalians," *www.wnd.com/news/article.asp?ARTICLE_ID=34083*, August 20, 2003.

2. Bill Fancher and Fred Jackson, "'Tolerance' of Homosexuality—Church Offers Confusing Stance," *www.headlines.agapepress.org*, August 15, 2003.

3. Jim Brown, "Christians Thrown Out: Baseball Execs Eject Biblical Message from Homosexual Event," *www.headlines.agapepress.org/users/worthynews/worthynews4.asp?*, August 18, 2003.

4. Dallas, p. 21

5. "Conclusion: No Law Against Love," *www.jesusmcc.org/freespirit/not08.html*, August 27, 2003.

Chapter 9

1. Dailey, *Dark Obsession*, p. 6.

2. Dallas, pp. 7–8.

3. Ibid., pp. 9–10.

4. Jeffrey Satinover, M.D., "The Gay Gene?" *www.family.org*, July 3, 2003, p. 2.

5. Ibid.

6. Dallas, p. 11

7. Satinover, *Homosexuality*, pp. 245–246.

8. Ibid., p. 234.

9. Dailey, *Dark Obsession*, p. 49.

Postscript

1. Dallas, p. 3.